TEAM EVANGELISM

Outreach for the 90% who don't have the gift of Evangelism

Larry Gilbert

Church Growth Institute

Providing Practical Tools for Growth
P.O. Box 4404, Lynchburg, VA 24502

Editor: Cindy G. Spear
Designer: Carolyn R. Phelps
Editorial and
Design Assistants: Tamara Johnson
Lisa Livingston

First Printing, June 1991
Second Printing, February 1992
Third Printing, April 1992
Fourth Printing, April 1993
TEAM Evangelism is a registered trademark of Church Growth Institute
Printed in the United States of America
ISBN 0-941005-35-6

CONTENTS

PREFACE

TEAM Evangelism is *not* a traditional, personal evangelism program. It is *not* a program for training Christians how to present the Gospel. It is *not* a program on how to do visitation. **TEAM Evangelism represents a whole new philosophy for lay evangelism.** It is based on the *TEAM Philosophy of Ministry* – using people where they are usable. It is a strategy for organizing yourself and structuring your church to do effective outreach. Its nontraditional approach and low-keyed tactics are not designed to fit the clergy, but to fit the *ordinary Christian*.[1] In fact, *TEAM Evangelism* specifically appeals to the 90 percent of church members who do not have the gift of evangelism.

In 1989, more than 12,000 new products were introduced to the American public. Of those products, more than 80 percent failed. Expert business consultants believe that the reason for this high failure rate lies with businessmen developing products without first finding out what the consumer wants and needs. They develop products based on *their own* wants and needs. Therefore, the consumer doesn't buy. Granted, the businessmen *think* they know what the consumer needs, but the facts show that 80 percent of the time, they are wrong.

Like the blinded businessmen, we (meaning most local church denominational and parachurch leaders) too are developing without considering the wants and needs of our users. We have long recognized that to get the job done we must utilize the laity. We fail to recognize that we need to change our methods to fit the laity.

Most personal evangelism programs were written by men with the gift of evangelism: pastors, evangelists, soulwinners, seminary professors, seminary presidents, or denominational executives; men who rose to the top and became leaders in their fields. Unlike the people they lead, these men are far from being ordinary Christians or average laymen. Many of them have never been laymen in their adult lives. Often unable to relate to the average Christian, these men developed methods designed to fit people like themselves and imposed them on everyone. No wonder we have problems getting people involved in evangelism! Research indicates that only 10 percent of church members are like these men in that they have the gift of evangelism. They are outgoing, confrontational, and driven to win the world for Christ. They can comfortably present the Gospel to strangers as well as people they already know. The majority of materials written on evangelism are useful to this minority of Christians. Then what about the other 90 percent who do not have this gift? Why not provide a method that fits them and allows them to effectively work with the other 10 percent – a method that does not force them to become someone they're not.

TEAM Evangelism is designed to fit the gifts and personalities of the 90 percent of Christians who do not have the gift of evangelism. *TEAM Evangelism* is lay oriented and written from a lay perspective for the ordinary Christian. It can truly be called "user-friendly," because it is not written as a program for other people to use – it is written by and for those who will use it.

I am not advocating changing the Gospel to fit people nor am I embracing a social Gospel; *the message of the Gospel is changeless.* However, I believe it is time to evaluate the effect our methods have on the work force who attempts to use them.

The term *TEAM* in *TEAM Evangelism* does not imply a visitation team of three or four people. It stands for "people working together for the benefit of the whole" and has several connotations in *TEAM Evangelism.*

1. *Christians teamed with Christians:* All the members of the local church work and cooperate to carry out the responsibilities given to the church.

2. *Spiritual gifts teamed with spiritual gifts:* In 1 Corinthians 12, Paul uses a three-way analogy indicating that the members of the body of Christ (the church) are not only Christians but are also the various spiritual gifts possessed by those Christians. Plus, Ephesians 4:16 indicates that the gifts fitted properly equal numeric and spiritual growth.

3. *Laity teamed with leadership: TEAM Evangelism* develops a partnership between clergy and laity by recognizing that each plays a different role. It utilizes the role of the *Ephesians 4 Pastor:* the steward of the gifts, talents, and abilities of those entrusted to his care. Therefore, the pastor leads, trains, and encourages while the laity performs the work of the ministry.

4. *The church teamed with God:* Based on 1 Corinthians 3:9, "For we are labourers together with God," the church carries out the role given to it while God fulfills the promises given to the church.

5. *Methods teamed with methods: TEAM Evangelism* recognizes that many different methods used over the years are valid and have a

place in most churches. Many methods, although incomplete or representative of select groups, actually complement each other when used cooperatively.

6. *People teamed with methods:* TEAM Evangelism acknowledges that of the many different methods for reaching people for Christ, some are more suitable for some people than others. *TEAM Evangelism* helps the individual identify the method that will be most suitable to him or her.

A note to the pastor: This is a lay-oriented textbook. It is written by laypeople for laypeople. However, there are four stages to developing an effective evangelism program. 1) Philosophy, 2) Principles and Laws, 3) Application of the Principles and Laws, and 4) Implementation of the Application into the Church. (These stages will be addressed further in chapter two.) All four of these stages require your leadership.

I find it imperative to stress to the pastor the need for implementing this entire philosophy in your church. The *TEAM Mate* book and this textbook make up three-fourths of the program, but only one-fourth of its potential effectiveness. It will have only minimal effectiveness without full involvement of the church. (See Appendix 3 for a list of the resources available to help you implement TEAM Evangelism in your church.)

My sincere prayer is that *TEAM Evangelism* will help your church grow both numerically and spiritually.

Larry Gilbert
Lynchburg, Virginia

FOOTNOTES

[1] The term "ordinary Christian" in no way denotes a belittling of the laity. Other terms denoting the same are laity, average Christian, man/woman in the pew, everyday Christian, nonseminary student, nonprofessional, normal Christian, and so on.

SECTION ONE

PREPARING FOR
THE TASK

Introduction

GAINING FREEDOM FROM PESKY PRESUPPOSITIONS

I once attended a high school play where the stage was set without removing all the scenery from the previous play. About one-third through the production someone realized the old scenery was still there and dropped a curtain between the old backdrop and the new settings. Once I realized the old scenery had nothing to do with the new play, the new play began to take on a whole new meaning. Until that point I was confused.

The same is true when teaching principles. Sometimes the stage must be cleared before it is set. And the stage of evangelism is loaded with a lot of unnecessary scenery in the form of *presuppositions* left over from former dramas of evangelism in past years. These presuppositions create barriers for people attempting to conduct effective outreach. *It is not what you are that holds you back, it is what you think you're not* – and when it comes to evangelism and outreach, most Christians believe *they are not* capable of reaching people for Christ. Problems arise when people take the teachings of evangelism and incorporate them with their feelings. Thus, they constantly think that they need to perform like someone else. Failure only leads to guilt, which becomes counterproductive in the process of reaching people for Christ.

What Are Presuppositions?

First let me define a presupposition. A presupposition is an assumption, something taken for granted; a deduction lacking direct evidence. Before I further explain TEAM Evangelism, I want to get rid of some of those pesky presuppositions, and expose them for what they really are – "guilt-makers" and barriers to evangelism.

1. *Any Christian who is willing to commit himself or herself, can become a dynamic soulwinner, skillfully able to meet total strangers and lead them to Christ.* Truthfully, not everyone is going to be able to develop into a door-to-door evangelist or street preacher. Only the Christian with the *gift of evangelism* can effectively do this. However, all Christians can use their own God-given gifts in the process of evangelism and can help stair-step people to Christ.

   There was a time when I might have had to spend a lot of time arguing the point that there is a *gift* of evangelism. Thankfully, today, most people believe that God has given a gift to certain people that allows them to be more aggressive, confrontational, and outgoing in their witnessing. The gifted evangelist can lead people to Christ far easier than the average Christian. Nearly 10 percent of all church members have this special gift.[1] This book is really not written for those people who have the gift of evangelism. In fact, one of the largest problems with educational material on evangelism is that most personal evangelism books are written by, and unfortunately only for, people with the gift of evangelism.

The purpose of this book is to help the remaining 90 percent of the church, those people *without* the gift of evangelism, become the kind of witnesses God wants them to be. *TEAM Evangelism* will show every member of the church that they can play an effective part in influencing people for Christ without having to become super-aggressive, outgoing or confrontational, and without having to become anyone other than themselves. They only have to be the person God has created them to be. All they need to do is use the gifts and abilities that God has already given them.

2. *I need to participate in an intense, repetitive training program before I can effectively share Christ with others.* In fact, most evangelism programs are based on the belief that the reason people are not evangelizing is lack of training. Some programs run as long as 16 weeks.

   TEAM Evangelism requires neither lengthy nor repetitive training sessions. In fact, it does not require "training" at all. Participants do not need to memorize dozens of Scripture passages or answers to objections. Nor do they need to take a lengthy soul-winning course before they qualify to effectively reach out to others. *TEAM Evangelism* requires only a simple understanding of its principles and an explanation of the application.

3. *I must increase my level of spirituality before I can effectively share Christ with others.* If we could measure spirituality on a scale of one to ten, where would you be? Realistically no one would be a "10." Regardless of where anyone would be, most people at one time or another were convinced that before they could effectively share Christ they had to become more spiritual than they were. This way of thinking means that if someone is a 3, before that person can become a good witness, he or she needs to become a 5. Another person may start off as a 5 and after going

through a discipleship program he or she becomes a 7. My question is, if the person who started off as a 3 and moved up to a 5 is now qualified, why wasn't the person who started off as a 5 and moved up to a 7 qualified in the beginning?

I am not at all suggesting that it is unnecessary for all Christians to grow spiritually nor am I putting down discipleship training. On the contrary, this is a must. But what I am suggesting is that a higher level of spirituality should never be a prerequisite or a barrier for not sharing Christ with others. Of course, the exception would be anyone with problems so obvious that they would cause reproach to the name of Christ. Let's face it, some people could do more for the cause of Christ if the unsaved did not know they were Christians.

TEAM Evangelism only requires participants to understand their relationship to the Spirit of God, the nature of evangelism itself, and the use of the particular witnessing method with which they are comfortable.

4. *"Spiritual" Christians are concerned about the spiritual well-being of casual acquaintances and strangers.* Factually, they are not. However, I'm not saying they shouldn't be concerned about the guy at the gas station or the stranger seated next to them on an airplane, I'm just pointing out the way it is. Any evangelistic program that uses the argument of "a lost and dying world, going to hell" as its motivation is ignored by many people, because generally people don't really care about casual acquaintances, let alone strangers. However, people do care for those within their own sphere of influence: unsaved family, friends, neighbors, and associates. They will pray for and work harder to win familiar people to Christ than they will for strangers. Christians are more likely to invite neighbors to an event where they have opportunity to hear the Gospel than they are to invite an unknown bank cashier. The truth is that *everyone cares more for some people than others because of existing, established relationships which developed over the years.*

People improve their potential for effective witnessing by concentrating on those with whom they regularly communicate – the ones who are most receptive to them, their church, and their Saviour. *TEAM Evangelism* keys in on these relationships, thus making ordinary Christians far more effective by easily allowing them to reach out to these receptive people.

5. *The longer I am a Christian, the fewer unchurched friends I will
   have, until finally all my friends are church-attending Christians.*
   Many people believe they cannot do any form of Lifestyle Evangelism because the people they have relationships with are saved.
   Therefore, all they have left to reach are strangers.

   TEAM Evangelism will show you that everyone, regardless of
   how long they have been a Christian, has relationships with an average of seven unchurched people who are potential members for
   their church. *TEAM Evangelism* includes a simple method that allows you to easily identify these personal prospects.

6. *Sharing Christ with someone should be a "now-or-never" decision-making situation.* Some Christians believe a person has not even
   witnessed unless he or she has presented the Gospel and pressed
   for a decision. Although the average life span in America is 73
   years, most Christians are taught to present the Gospel like everyone is going to die tomorrow. The Bible does teach that "life is but
   a vapor" and we "know not what tomorrow holds" but pressing for
   an immediate decision often builds barriers that prevent people
   from accepting Christ. Even worse, *it builds barriers in Christians
   that prevent them from even presenting the Gospel.*

   TEAM Evangelism offers a method for introducing people to
   Christ that is inoffensive to both the personal prospect and the presenter.

7. *Before I can share Christ with others, I must become sales-oriented and able to get a decision.* A person once stated, "Evangelism is one of the penalties for being a Christian." Many people
   view evangelism as a "when I build up enough nerve" program.
   They visualize programs with outlines like: 1) Present the facts;
   2) Picture the facts; 3) Prove the facts; 4) Press for the decision;
   5) Probe,[2] which helps keep their fear alive. Knowing that their
   personalities would never allow them to follow such an outline
   only leads to strengthening the barriers that already exist. Now
   they are sure they have to change and become like someone else to
   share Christ effectively.

   TEAM Evangelism allows *all* Christians to be themselves and
   be effective and inoffensive in reaching others for Christ.

The Bottom Line

The bottom line: Would you be a witness for Christ if you did not have to become someone else to do it? Would you be a witness if you did not have to pressure someone into a decision for Christ? Would you be a witness if you did not have to participate in an intense, prolonged training program? *Would you be a witness if you could just be yourself?*

Most people do not make any attempt to evangelize because they fear rejection. Many times they never attempt to share Christ with someone simply because they feel that they do not have the personality needed in order to use a method that someone else has convinced them is the only way that will work.

I remember a time several years ago when an evangelist and the pastor of my home church were trying to motivate our members to "go out and win the lost." A young lady in my Sunday School class told me, "If they think I'm going to go out and get people saved, they're crazy, because I just can't do it." Yet that very evening, she and her husband were responsible for having 26 visitors in the service. Several of them accepted Christ during the invitation. Was she an evangelist or not? Yes? No?[3] The important point was that *she did not think she was.* However, she was doing as Paul exhorted in 2 Timothy 4:5, where he says, "Do the work of an evangelist." Her problem was that she was not doing it through direct confrontation which she *thought* was expected of her and which she *thought* was the only way that counts.

The goal of this book is to help you "do the work of an evangelist" through utilizing the gifts God has given you.

In a Nutshell

Presuppositions are barriers to people doing effective outreach. When people feel like they must do something with which they are uncomfortable in order to participate in a program or activity, they tend to avoid it altogether. Often they feel guilty for not doing those things that are contradictory to their personalities or that do not fit their own giftedness (possession of particular gifts given by God according to His discernment).

TEAM Evangelism shows every member of the church how they can effectively influence people for Christ without having to become anyone but themselves. All they need to do is use their own God-given gifts and abilities. Some people are aggressive and confrontational because God has given them the gift of evangelism, but 90 percent of church members do not have this gift. *TEAM Evangelism* will help everyone in the church work in harmony with the evangelist, using the individual gifts God has given them to influence others for Christ.

TEAM MATE INSTRUCTIONS

The accompanying *TEAM Mate* book interacts with the *TEAM Evangelism* text. Once you have read the text, *TEAM Mate* serves as the tool to help you apply the principles of *TEAM Evangelism*. It also serves as a refresher as it briefly covers the information in this text. Once a month review the principles in the front; by doing so you will gain new enlightenment to the application. Please open *TEAM Mate* to the title page and fill in your name and address. Notice that the introduction on page 3 recaps this introduction. Page 5 gives instructions on how to use *TEAM Mate*. Turn to page 7 and fill in the information about your church team.

FOOTNOTES

[1] Approximately 10 percent of all church members have the gift of evangelism. Therefore, 90 percent of all members do not have the gift. This estimate is based on the evaluation of thousands of spiritual gift inventories given over the years by the author. However, others who have written on this subject estimate as little as 1 to 3 percent have the gift of evangelism. The author's observation is, that of the total evaluated, 4 to 5 percent have evangelism as their dominant (number 1) gift while 5 to 6 percent have it as a secondary or number two gift. Differences in opinion may be attributed to the fact that of those people with the gift of evangelism, only a small percent actually use the gift in public view. However, when tested a much larger number are recognizable.

[2] Lord, Jack: Evangelism, Person to Person: Reaching the World with the Gospel.

[3] Technically, the young lady in the illustration was not an evangelist. An evangelist is one who proclaims the Gospel; it denotes a preacher of the Gospel (Acts 21:8). It is also noteworthy that in 2 Timothy 4:5 Paul did not exhort Timothy to "be" an evangelist, but to simply "do the work of an evangelist." The function of the latter can easily be defined as "witnessing" or "sharing."

Chapter 1

UNDERSTANDING THE TASK

The church I grew up in taught me that the greatest responsibility given to the church is to meet the needs of people – to help the sick, the poor, those who have experienced tragedy – church members as well as those outside the church. Then when I went away to college, the church I attended stressed soulwinning, getting people saved, as its greatest responsibility. After graduating, I settled down in a new community and joined a church that taught discipleship as the church's purpose. They believed in teaching people what the Bible had to say about living the Christian life. Now, because of a job transfer, I'm searching for a new church home. What will my new church stress as the church's greatest responsibility? Which one is right? I'm confused.

Sound familiar? Have you ever really considered the question, Just what is the church's primary task?

Although we could find a number of Scriptures that explain the responsibility God has given to the church – no passage expresses it as clearly and completely as the Great Commission. In fact the Great Commission has been said to be the greatest command, given by the greatest Commander, to the greatest army, for the greatest task ever. If we are to fulfill that task, it is necessary for us to understand it. Let's examine that task.

The Real Task

Go ye therefore and teach all nations, baptizing them in the name of the Father and of the Son and of the Holy Ghost, teaching them to observe all things whatsoever I have commanded you: And, lo, I am with you alway, even until the end of the world (Matt. 28:19-20).

For years we have accepted the Great Commission as our marching order to evangelize the world. We are taught our job is to *seek* and to *save*. We accept the responsibility to reach out to the lost, to become soulwinners and send thousands into third world countries as missionaries. We go from door to door, preach on street corners, pass out tracts, paint "Jesus Saves" on billboards, and confront millions of strangers with the Gospel.

Yet, at the same time, many who take the fulfillment of this Great Commission to heart wonder why numerous others are so lackadaisical when it comes to getting involved. Is it possible that in our haste, zeal, and burden to fulfill the Great Commission we have come short in the interpretation of it? We have always said the Great Commission is the command to evangelize the world – to get people saved, to lead people to Christ. But is it possible that the salvation of the lost is only part of the Great Commission, and by failing to recognize this fact we have limited our vision, limited our goals, and driven away much of the work force that God has given to fulfill His Great Commission?

As we look at this Great Commission, I believe the real task goes beyond the traditional belief of evangelism. From youth, I have been taught that this command was given to me, individually, charging me with the responsibility to lead the lost to Christ. I now believe the real Commission goes further than that. The task is given to the church to reach the lost, assimilate them into the body of Christ, and train them to become Christlike. In order for the church to do this, it must recognize that the fulfillment of the Great Commission is not a single event – but a *process* that encompasses several different events taking place over a period of time. It starts by our appealing to individuals who in many cases have only a superficial awareness of God, then stepping them through a growth process with the objective of them becoming Christlike.

The Great Commission: A Process

The Great Commission is a process which includes the event of salvation as well as many steps leading up to and beyond salvation (sometimes called preconversion, conversion, and post-conversion or pre-evangelism, evangelism, and post-evangelism). These steps in developing maturity in the individual involve a ministry that utilizes the various spiritual gifts of all church members. The entire body of Christ needs to participate in the process of the Great Commission. The examination of three key words (*teach, nations, baptize*) in the context of the Commission reveals this process to us.

Go ye therefore and **teach**. The first word we want to look at is *teach* or *mathetevo* (Gk.). The Greek word literally means *to make disciples of*. Today when a person gets saved we call him a *Christian*. When he matures beyond just being a pew sitter and really attempts to accomplish something for Christ we recognize him as a *disciple*. However, in New Testament times it was the opposite. When someone accepted the teaching of Christ and became a follower of Christ, he became a *disciple* (a follower). The name Christian came later when disciples were first called Christians in Antioch, *after* they had become imitators or Christlike. This suggests that we are to reach people and lead or influence them to become disciples first, then teach them to become Christians. Making disciples in Scripture is *getting people saved.* (However, let's not get hung up on terminology. Some would argue, using today's meaning of *disciple*, that the Commission is not a command to evangelize but to make disciples, with the term "disciple" encompassing the whole procedure of the Commission. This offers no threat to *TEAM Evangelism.* In application, both arrive at the same destination.)

All nations. These two words in the Great Commission give us an insight as to whom Jesus was giving the Great Commission. In an effort to get everyone involved in evangelism, many argue that the Great Commission was given to the individual, not to the church as a corporate body; therefore, every individual in the church must literally fulfill the Great Commission. If this were true, it would be an impossible task. There are 169 nations and five billion people in the world today. If the Commission were given to me as an *individual* would I be responsible to reach every nation on the face of the earth by myself? How can any individual "take the Gospel; to every creature"? That is why the Great Commission is given to the *church. Only the church with its many members using their various gifts and abilities, working together as a team, can fulfill the Great Commission.*

Baptizing them. These two words destroy the argument of many people who say that the Great Commission is given to the individual; because they also say, "The individual does not have the authority to baptize." Although opinions differ on this, most agree that God gave this authority only to the church. We must examine this in the context of the whole Great Commission. If the authority to baptize is given only to the church and that authority is given in the middle of the Commission, then the whole Commission is given to the church to be fulfilled as a corporate body where people fulfill it as part of a team, not individually.

Baptizing them in the name of the Father, and of the Son, and of the Holy Ghost. This is the second part of the procedure of reaching lost people for Christ. Doctrinally we may argue whether baptism is submersion or sprinkling but functionally we all agree it equals *iden-*

tification with the body of Christ or the local church. *It is not enough simply to lead people to Christ. They should become active members, involved in the ministry, fellowship, education, worship, and stewardship of the local church.* Baptizing is getting people churched. "Go out into the highways and hedges and compel them to come in, that my house may be filled" (Luke 14:23). At the risk of nagging you, I will continually emphasize this point throughout this text because of its importance and because of its relationship to *all* the principles of effective evangelism.

Continuing in verse 20. ***Teaching*** *them to observe all things, whatsoever I have commanded you.* In this last verse we see that the fulfilling or the third part of the procedure of the Great Commission is to *teach.* Here the word *teach* is translated from a different Greek word than used in verse 19. *Didasko* (Gk) means to *teach* or to *give instruction* which is the same way we would define teach today. Christ gives the command to teach them (the world) to observe all *things* that He commanded. *All things* takes in the entire content of the Scriptures. It takes in every area of our lives, not just the spiritual aspects but the daily aspects as well. Jesus spoke of money, of relationships to our spouses, of our relationship to Him, of prayer life, and so forth. This is part of developing a mature Christian. This *is being Christlike which is the third part of the Great Commission.*

Two Major Principles

In summary, the Great Commission communicates two major principles:

1. The Great Commission is more than a single function that stops with the event of someone's salvation. It is more than just a command to evangelize the world. It is a *process* by which we evangelize, reach the unchurched who are usually lost (not Christians), make them aware of their sin, and lead them step-by-step closer to accepting Christ. The event of conversion is when they go from darkness to light and identify themselves with the local church through baptism. The procedure does not stop there. It continues as we instruct them in all the things the Bible teaches us. They must learn to become Christlike. The Scripture commands us, the church, to reach, baptize, and teach. The functional command tells us to lead them to Christ, get them churched, and bring them to maturity in Christ.

Even still we must recognize two important things: (1) No individual will ever become totally Christlike. However, we should never set a goal of anything less. (2) No individual who only has a superficial awareness of God can become Christlike without experiencing the event of salvation. We must also recognize that this is only one part of the procedure and to stop short of the goal to become Christlike will leave an individual spiritually incomplete.

2. Rarely do people recognize that the Great Commission only tells us *what to do* and *who* is to do it, **not** *how* to do it. Many scholars think that for the most part the Bible is void of methodology. This leaves each generation free to develop a methodology that is relevant to the culture to which it ministers. This does not mean that a methodology can be developed without adhering to biblical principles. It does mean that we do not have to imitate every movement of those who did successful evangelism in the Scriptures or in the last century or even in the last decade. (This will be the subject of Chapter 2 in this text.)

Expanding the Commission from traditional views has not limited it or added barriers to it, but in reality simplified its potential for fulfillment. *TEAM Evangelism* recognizes that in order for the church to fulfill the Great Commission, a broad spectrum of talents, gifts, and abilities are required. Surely God has not given every Christian the many gifts required to do all of the functions to carry out this procedure. In rarely is a single individual strong in several, let alone all, of these functions. But God has given us an organism containing many different, gifted individuals who can excel in the various areas required to fulfill the complete process of the Great Commission. We call this group of people *the church*, the *TEAM*. Dr. Charles Arn writes, "The local church – with its complementary assortment of spiritual gifts – more accurately reflects the body of Christ than any one individual member."[1]

In a Nutshell

The *task* of the Great Commission is more than a command to evangelize. It is a process that encompasses pre-conversion, conversion, and post-conversion. We must lead people to Christ, but we must also influence them to identify with the local church – to become active members – and instruct them in all the things the Bible has taught us, so they can grow into mature Christians.

To fulfill the Great Commission, TEAM *Evangelism* incorporates the broad spectrum of talents, gifts, and abilities God has given each of us. We work together using our strengths as a united team to reach, baptize, and teach others for Him.

TEAM MATE INSTRUCTIONS

See page 8 of TEAM *Mate* for a brief review of this chapter.

FOOTNOTES

[1] Wagner, Peter C.; Arn, Charles; Towns, Elmer, *Church Growth State of the Art* (Tyndale House Publishers, Inc. : 1986), Page 61.

Chapter One

REVIEW QUESTIONS

1. What is the Great Commission?

2. What is the biblical difference between a Christian and a disciple?

3. To whom was the Great Commission given?

DISCUSSION QUESTIONS

1. As team members of the local church, what must we do to fulfill the Great Commission?

2. Is your church fulfilling the Great Commission? How or why not?

3. What can you as an individual do to help fulfill the Great Commission?

Chapter 2

UNDERSTANDING THE METHOD

Recently I had a discussion with an acquaintance who expressed his dismay with a church he had joined by mistake. He told me, "My wife and I moved into town from Texas. We looked around and visited a number of churches in the area. Finally, we found one that we felt comfortable in. After attending five or six services we felt the friendliness, warmth, and concern for us, so we joined. Shortly after joining we were asked to attend their new members class. This is where our problem started. The new members class was an excellent orientation to their church. It taught the basic doctrines and the church's philosophy of ministry. It was all well received and fitting – until they came to the class on Personal Evangelism. I could not believe the cockamamy scheme they devised for outreach, and then had the nerve to call it 'evangelism.' Well, it didn't take us long to see the light. Now we are checking out all the churches again – and this time you can rest assured that we're going to check out the evangelism program first. This time we are going to select a church that does evangelism the way we are taught in the Scriptures. We want a church that does it the way the Bible says to do it."

Is this man right in thinking there is only one way to evangelize? Does the Bible tell us exactly how to do it? Have you ever searched to find if Scripture mandates the *method* we are to use?

A Misconception

One of the largest misconceptions plaguing evangelism is people's inability to separate the mandate (command) from the method (procedure or technique for doing). As stated in the previous chapter, the Great Commission gives us a mandate of *what* we should do (lead people to salvation in Christ, get them churched, and train them to be Christlike) and *who* should do it (the church), but not *how* to do it. Or another way of putting it, Jesus told us what He wants us to do and who should do it, but He never gave us a method for doing it.

If the Great Commission tells us *what* to do and *who* is to do it, not *how* to do it; then the *what* and *who* is the command that spans over all of time and the *how* is the method that must fit the cultures existing within different periods of time.

Therefore, it disturbs me to see people developing *a method* for evangelism, then presenting it as *the* method. I find it unbelievable to think that God has been playing games with us by hiding the "true methodology" of evangelism in the Scriptures and leaving us for centuries to try to find it. One author suggests this by describing the effectiveness of the method Jesus used. He states, "He did it so well that it took us 2,000 years to realize what He had done."[1] On the next page he suggests the reason it took so long to discover this was because it took someone like himself who is not so professional to recognize it.

I am convinced that if we could determine the exact methodology that was used in Scripture, at best, we would have a methodology that was 2,000 years old. I believe we can safely say that Jesus, Paul, and any other person who evangelized during Bible years used the methodology that fit the culture of the first century. We can learn much by studying it, but we don't need to imitate it in every way.

Developing Effective Methods

TEAM Evangelism is not another program to train Christians how to do visitation, nor is it a program for training Christians on how to present the Gospel. *TEAM Evangelism* represents a complete new philosophy of ministry. It provides a totally new school of thought concerning evangelism and suggests a uniquely different method of application from previous Personal Evangelism programs.

A *method* is an orderly arrangement or plan: a procedure for achieving an end. There are four stages to developing an effective evangelism methodology. 1) Philosophy, 2) Principles and Laws, 3) Application of the Principles and Laws, and 4) Implementation of the Application into the Church. A closer look at each of these points will show how a method is developed:

1. *Philosophy*. Philosophy basically states your fundamental and foundational beliefs, concepts, and attitudes, your sum of personal convictions. Philosophy is the starting point for any and all teaching.

2. *Principles and Laws*. As we study, teach, question, research, and gather data, we examine that data, suggest a hypothesis and test the hypotheses to determine principles and laws. These fundamental laws govern our conduct and practices.

3. *Application of Principles and Laws*. Principles and Laws are useless if someone does not form a way to put them to practical use.

This is application. We must be able to use our principles by employing them in everyday life. Without application the best of principles will never get results.

4. *Implementation of the Application into the Church.* This point may seem a play on words because we often use the words *application* and *implementation* interchangeably. However, we are not talking about implementing the principles and laws but implementing their application. This means that once we have learned to apply these principles we must put them in practice through the local church. Remember, the Great Commission was given to the *church* not the *individual*, therefore if the principles are applied only by the individual it leaves the church and the individual functioning in isolation from one another. *For any method to be effective it must have leadership, organization, structure, harmony, correlation, coordination, control, and accountability.* These things can be fulfilled only by putting the application under the umbrella of the local church.

History of Personal Evangelism

A short history lesson explaining from where Personal Evangelism has come, where it is today, and where it is headed will help you understand the dominant methods that exist today. You will need this information to properly understand the method that TEAM *Evangelism* uses.

First, let me explain what I mean by *Personal Evangelism.* The New Testament gives examples of *two* very definite types of evangelism – Mass Evangelism and Personal Evangelism.[2] Mass Evangelism for the most part is bringing large groups of people to where one or a handful of people present the Gospel to them. These gatherings are most often referred to as "revivals" or "evangelistic campaigns." Men like Wesley, Finney, Moody, Rice, and more recently, Billy Graham have used this method very effectively. Since "Mass Evangelism" is not the method TEAM *Evangelism* uses, I do not want to spend any further time on it other than to recognize it as a valid method. I support Mass Evangelism and feel that we should continue to use it whenever and wherever possible. However, it does not use laypeople like Personal Evangelism does.

Personal Evangelism is not using a handful to reach a lot, but is evangelism being done at the lay level, usually one-on-one, using everyday, ordinary Christians like you and me. In fact, because Personal

Evangelism mostly involves *laypeople* evangelizing others, the method has recently been termed *Lay* Evangelism. Lay Evangelism is the most suitable term for *TEAM Evangelism*.

Here's where the surprise comes in – most of us non-historians think that because the New Testament gives examples of Lay Evangelism and because we put such great emphasis on it today, Lay Evangelism has always been a method of evangelism. It has not. By the third century A.D., New Testament evangelism (mass and personal or lay) was lost in the theological controversy that thrust the church into the Dark Ages.

Confrontational Evangelism

Although Mass Evangelism was revived in the middle 1700s no real revival of Lay Evangelism came until 1897 when R. A. Torrey wrote the book, *Leading Men to Christ*. This book began the formation of a whole new philosophy in evangelism – *Confrontational Evangelism*. This philosophy basically conveys the idea that every Christian has the responsibility to witness to every unsaved person. Furthermore, witnessing goes beyond the personal testimony, requiring the individual to present the plan of salvation and pursue a decision. (I recognize that in 1897 and the years following it was not called "Confrontational Evangelism." This title was given to it later by its opponents. Although the name originated as a put-down, many who hold this philosophy wear the title with pride because it represents their basic foundational beliefs.)

During the 60 years following the release of Torrey's book, numerous other books were written. They all had one thing in common – an 80% overlap with Torrey's philosophy. This philosophy grew fast and wide because it was also being taught in every Bible institute, Bible college, and seminary throughout North America and Europe.

Evangelism Explosion Emerges

Although these new books supported Torrey's philosophy and expanded on the principles and laws, no real results were seen in Lay Evangelism until the 1920s when several denominations developed Sunday School enrollment and visitation activities that incorporated the principles. However, the largest impact on the church came in the early 1960s when D. James Kennedy wrote the book *Evangelism Explosion* (*EE*). *EE* crossed all denominational barriers and became an instant success because it was more than a book, it was a systematic program. Although many books had been written on the subject, no one had developed a systematic program that would give application to the principles and put them under the authority of the local church. Until *EE* was published, people read the books and tried to utilize the principle being taught in them, but nothing tied their efforts directly to the church. When *EE* was introduced it provided training along with a vehicle for application (organized visitation) which actually involved laypeople. It began to get measurable results.

EE equipped churches with a training program that 1) taught the philosophy, 2) taught the principles and laws, 3) trained people to overcome obstacles in presenting the Gospel, 4) provided the church with an organized program that put it at the center of the efforts of its members, 5) provided an outlet for the expression of what they were being trained for: "Thursday night visitation," and 6) involved the laity.

What Kennedy had done was put Confrontational Evangelism directly into stage four. The philosophy and principles were already there. *EE* simply added application and implementation.

This success started a whole new writing campaign. Now Kennedy's "program" was literally being "perfected" by a new phenomena – publishers, denominations, and evangelists. Publishers offered a competing product while each denomination developed their own version. At the same time many evangelists developed their own programs because each had a little different twist to make it more successful.

Although these evangelists closely adhered to the same philosophy, many took *EE's* application and used it in door-to-door and citywide campaigns. This evolution not only gave a new meaning to visitation; it pulled the application away from the local church.

Lifestyle Evangelism: An Alternative

Thus, a new philosophy began to peek over the horizon. Some Christians obviously did not fit into the methodology that the confrontational philosophy was developing. Many people feared going to the training programs, let alone doing evangelism the way the training programs taught them. Plus they observed the problems, misuses and abuses that accompanied Confrontational Evangelism. This led to a new philosophy – *Lifestyle Evangelism*. Lifestyle Evangelism is a process for networking people into receptive, redemptive relationships. It is living your life that others might see Christ in you.

Unlike Confrontational Evangelism's teaching that every Christian needs to *present* the Gospel, Lifestyle Evangelism's philosophy says that every Christian needs to *live* the Gospel. It emphasizes developing relationships and networking them into the congregation with far less aggressive approaches.

Now the process that Confrontational Evangelism had gone through was repeating itself with Lifestyle Evangelism. Many new books expounded the philosophy of Lifestyle Evangelism. But with the church entering the information age, it had a new tool – research backed by oceans of statistics and the computer – to help it formulate new principles and laws .

Armed with the most up-to-date principles and laws, Lifestyle Evangelism finds itself in stage three today – developing application. Although many churches, denominations, parachurch organizations, and especially the church growth movement, have made great advances in applying these principles, we have yet to see a suitable vehicle that puts a workable application in the hands of the laity. Some have successfully utilized these principles in short-term programs such as attendance campaigns, but none have really made them work on an ongoing basis.

The real problem with Lifestyle Evangelism is in stage four, the implementation stage. To this point all application has been aimed at the individual believer and nothing has been done to assemble the body by bringing that application under the umbrella of the local church. Remember, God gave the Commission to the church; therefore, the church must be at the center for any application to work.

A New Philosophy Is Born

Once again a new philosophy is being formulated – *TEAM Evangelism*. *TEAM Evangelism* is using people where they are usable. Based on the *TEAM Philosophy of Ministry*, it recognizes that God has given every believer a unique spiritual gift that enables him or her to perform a task differently than anyone else. It believes that God gave some Christians the gift of evangelism which allows them to perform in a more outgoing or confrontational manner while He gave all Christians the responsibility or role to be a witness. *TEAM Evangelism* examines the dominant philosophies of evangelism and utilizes their strengths while doing all possible to minimize their weaknesses.

Strengths and Weaknesses

A chart at the end of this chapter offers an explanation of the strengths and weaknesses of both Confrontational Evangelism and

Lifestyle Evangelism and shows how *TEAM Evangelism* utilizes their strengths and minimizes their weaknesses. Also, I conclude the chapter with my comments on the more dominant strengths and weaknesses of both and *TEAM Evangelism's* position on them.

Strengths of Confrontational Evangelism:

1. *Puts the local church at the center of activity.* Since the introduction of programs like *EE,* Confrontational Evangelism has been supported with a structured, highly organized system with controls that puts all evangelistic efforts under the authority of the local church.

2. *Provides how-to training.* *EE*-type programs also provide adequate training to teach people how to deal with problems they will encounter while presenting the Gospel.

3. *Vehicle for application.* The visitation program has served as a vehicle for carrying out Confrontational Evangelism. This organized and structured program can bring people to it and send people from it.

4. *Verbalization of the Gospel.* Because of the strong emphasis on presenting the Gospel, Confrontational Evangelism taught us the importance of verbalizing the message of the Gospel.

Weaknesses of Confrontational Evangelism:

1. *Assumptions that all will fit.* One of the greatest blind spots in Confrontational Evangelism is the failure to recognize that it is basically a program written by people with the gift of evangelism for people with the gift of evangelism and unfortunately imposes the qualities and duties of an evangelist on all the people. Therefore, it takes a program that is suitable for 10 percent of the people and imposes it on 100 percent of the people.

2. *False decisions.* People who are led to Christ in the church are more apt to remain in the church and people who are led to Christ outside the church usually do not attend church on a regular basis. My observation and research done by others backs up this claim. One study shows that of 4,106 decisions for Christ, made outside of a church, only 125 became new church members.[3] The danger is that the programs that are able to report a massive amount of de-

cisions are not only leaving people unchurched, but in many cases are leaving people "thinking" they are saved. Is a person better off thinking he or she is saved (just because he or she prayed the sinner's prayer with someone) when he or she is not or would it be better if no one had presented the Gospel to that person in the first place? (I'll say more about this in chapter seven.) Therefore, any program that leads people to Christ in their homes without having an effective strategy for getting these people into the church could be accused of actually pulling people away from the church rather than to the church.

3. *People won't attend training.* The largest problem cited by proponents of Confrontational Evangelism is that people will not commit themselves to do the training. In most cases these pastors believe that if they could only get people to attend the training classes, they would be able to be effective evangelists. However, the reason only a few commit to training is because the training is suitable for only a small portion of the church. The remainder fear and reject it.

   This perception of training that has been cultivated by the Confrontational Evangelism-type program spills over into other programs as well, making it hard to get Christians to come to *any* type evangelistic training program because of their preconceived notions of how it will be enacted.

Strengths of Lifestyle Evangelism:

1. *Removes guilt.* Lifestyle Evangelism represents approximately 90 percent of the church population. By recognizing the gift of evangelism and removing themselves from it, individuals are free to be themselves – guilt is removed.

2. *Utilizes strength of the relationship.* Lifestyle Evangelism puts its emphasis on building and developing relationships with individuals. For the most part it recognizes that dealing with casual acquaintances and strangers has little or no lasting results.

3. *Promotes holy living.* By putting the believer at the center of the evangelism process Lifestyle Evangelism promotes living a life that not only is acceptable to Christ but is also a witness to other people.

Weaknesses of Lifestyle Evangelism:

1. *The sin nature of man*. This method's critics accuse it of putting all its emphasis on modeling the Christian life in order to lead people to accept Christ or to "get saved." We recognize this approach will not work because most Christians are guilty of what I call the "Potts principle." Years ago, a friend of mine, Cleaver Potts, was a professional baseball player. He was the catcher for Babe Ruth when Babe Ruth was the pitcher for the Baltimore Orioles. Potts was a lonely old man and to get people's attention would tell his "war stories" of playing ball with the "Babe." Once he got you hooked, he would add some humor. He would say, "Eighty-seven years old (as if he were getting ready to give you his philosophy of life), don't drink, smoke, cuss, chew, fool around with women." And then after a long pause and in a low drawn-out voice he would say, "S-o-m-e-t-i-m-e-s."

   The problem with Christians living their lives that others might see Christ in them is that most Christians are like Clever Potts. They don't drink, smoke, cuss, chew, or fool around with the opposite sex, "sometimes." In fact, based on research by George Barna of Barna Research Group, "To the average non-believer, Christians act no differently than anyone else."[4] I am not implying that we need to abandon witnessing because of such problems, but I do believe that we must recognize that any program based on the sinless perfection of the believer is doomed to failure. Nor am I implying that Lifestyle Evangelism is guilty of this. But it is *perception* we are dealing with, not the facts. And the accusation being made about Lifestyle Evangelism is influencing more Christians than the program itself.

2. *No vehicle for application*. For the most part Lifestyle Evangelism has not developed a vehicle for carrying the Gospel to the nonbeliever.

3. *Failure to verbalize*. Because of the reactionary emphasis to Confrontational Evangelism, many have embraced Lifestyle Evangelism. They feel that it provides them with a valid argument for not verbalizing their faith. "I don't have to speak up; therefore I don't have to face rejection." Lifestyle Evangelism is truly a comfort zone for many Christians.

4. *Not church centered*. The real drawback with Lifestyle Evangel-

ism is that it *does not involve the church.* How do you apply Life-style Evangelism? Bake an apple pie, mow someone's lawn, show people that you care; get them to believe in you so they will be more receptive to the Gospel while you look for the right op-portunity to present it. This approach is sound. However, it is be-ing practiced at an individual level only.[5] It utilizes the members of the body of Christ (church members) but it never assembles the body. Another way of putting it is that is uses the fingers; it uses the thumb; it uses the knuckles; it uses the wrist; it uses the palm; but it never uses the hand.

The pastor who adopts Lifestyle Evangelism as a basis for his ministry finds himself participating at the same level as his peo-ple. He must serve as a role model. This means that if the pastor wishes to maintain a Lifestyle Evangelism program he needs to bake an apple pie, mow someone's lawn, and show people he cares; the same as any other member of the church. This he should do, this he *must* do; but if this is all he does, he is not exercising his position of leadership which calls for him to be the steward of the gifts, talents, and abilities of his flock. He is not *leading* his people to do the work of the ministry, he is *doing* the work of the ministry. It is imperative that he involves his church, its members, and him-self in the proper roles.

Evaluation of Both Philosophies

Although a variety of Scriptures are used for their support, both philosophies view their interpretations of the Great Commission as their foundation (Matt. 28: 18-20, Mark 16:15-18, Luke 24:47-48, John 20:21-23, and Acts 1:8). While both have good scriptural arguments, I am sure neither side would agree with such a statement about the other.

Each philosophy fits the gifts, personalities, motivations, tempera-ments, character strengths and weaknesses of that particular group, therefore demanding that we recognize each for what it is – a *method*, not a scriptural mandate. They are methods that basically suit the dom-inant gifts of each group. As stated earlier, most Confrontational Evan-gelism programs have been written by people with the dominant gift of evangelism and most Lifestyle Evangelism programs have been written by people with the dominant gift of teaching.

Strengths of *TEAM Evangelism*:

1. *User friendly. TEAM Evangelism* is not designed to fit any one

personality or gift type but is designed to fit all laypeople where they are.

2. *Utilizes principles of effective evangelism.* It examines and effectively uses the principles from both Confrontational and Lifestyle Evangelism.

3. *Low pressure.* Instead of requiring intense pressure to be put on people all the time in order to get results, TEAM *Evangelism* is low keyed on an ongoing basis with occasional short bursts of intense pressure.

4. *No remaking of the individual is necessary.* TEAM *Evangelism* does not require anyone to use a gift that he or she does not have, nor does it require a person to perform at a spiritual level he or she has not obtained. It allows the individual to be himself or herself.

5. *Puts application in the hands of the laity.* It recognizes the Ephesians 4 Pastor as the steward of the gifts, talents, and abilities of those entrusted to his care. It acknowledges that the work of the ministry is to be done by the laity while the pastor leads.

6. *Utilizes every member of the body.* It recognizes that spiritual gifts make up the body; therefore, the body can only be assembled when all of the gifts are there and each member is doing what he or she is equipped to do.

**How TEAM *Evangelism* minimizes the weaknesses
of Confrontational and Lifestyle Evangelism:**

1. *No training required.* Only a simple understanding of the principles and an explanation of the application is required. A person only needs to be trained to do something they do not know how to do. Once you have learned to ride a bicycle you always know how. Likewise, all of the principles and applications of TEAM *Evangelism* are things all Christians already know how to do. All TEAM *Evangelism* does is organize them and put them in a systematic form that allows you to apply them. Once an individual understands the principles and is given a simple plan of implementation he or she realizes how simple it really is.

2. *Recognizes the gift of evangelism.* TEAM *Evangelism* recognizes that any program developed only to fit the gift of evangelism

would exclude 90 percent[6] of those people in the church. TEAM Evangelism does not exclude the gift of evangelism but incorporates it into the area where it will be most effective, thus complementing the team with this gift rather than holding back the rest of the team by imposing the function of the gift on them.

3. *Utilizes people where they are.* Although TEAM Evangelism promotes spiritual growth, it recognizes that, other than problem Christians, increased spirituality should not be a prerequisite to reaching out to others with the message of Christ.

4. *Local church is central.* The entire structure of the TEAM Evangelism strategy and system puts the local church at the heart of all of its implementation.

5. *Promotes sharing through natural communication.*[7] All requirements and necessities for a preset agenda or canned presentation have been removed. Christians share through everyday activities where we live, work, and play.

TEAM Evangelism recognizes that there have been literally scores of books written on Lay Evangelism. Most all of these books teach us a method but few ever call it a method. They either teach us directly or leave us to believe that this particular method is spelled out in Scripture. Therefore, two things are happening: 1) People are taught only one method of evangelism and they believe it to be the scriptural way. Their inability to discipline themselves to function in the manner required causes them to experience guilt or lapse into complacency. 2) Many people have been taught several different methods of evangelism, or picked them up on their own, and are confused.

TEAM Evangelism claims only to be another method for doing outreach. However, it does not expel the other methods. It recognizes and utilizes the strengths of Confrontational Evangelism and at the same time recognizes and utilizes the strengths of Lifestyle Evangelism. The problem has not been the existence of different philosophies but the adversary attitude that exists between them. The bottom line of the TEAM Evangelism method is that it utilizes these other methods by incorporating them into the overall team.

In a Nutshell

Many people mistakenly believe that there is only one right way –

one method for reaching the lost. God gave the church the mandate to lead people to salvation in Christ, get them churched, and train them to be Christlike, but He gave us freedom to choose the method that best suits the individuals involved and best works in a given culture.

TEAM Evangelism is a strategy whereby team members work together using a method suitable to each individual to network people into the church and lead them to Christ, then on to become mature Christians. The evangelist is still allowed to be confrontational while the mercy-shower, exhorter, teacher, shepherd, etc., plays a different role in reaching out to the lost and unchurched. No one is forced into a mold in which they do not fit. Everyone has their own place.

TEAM Evangelism involves the whole church. As team members use their strengths and abilities in an organized process to reach others, they are working together in harmony toward their goal of leading people to Christ. For the most part, Confrontational Evangelism fits leadership while Lifestyle Evangelism is geared more toward laity.

TEAM MATE INSTRUCTIONS

Page 10 of *TEAM Mate* contains a brief review of this chapter.

FOOTNOTES

[1] Bryson, O.J., *Networking the Kingdom* (Word, Inc., Dallas, Texas), Page 35.

[2] A partial list of evangelism methods or types existing today are: Door-to-Door Evangelism, Saturation Evangelism, Oikos Evangelism, Evangelism Explosion, Front-Door Evangelism, Side-door Evangelism, Visitation Evangelism, Threshold Evangelism, Bussing Evangelism, Crusade Evangelism, Personal Evangelism, Mass Evangelism, Media Evangelism, Televangelism, Superaggressive Evangelism, Proclamation Evangelism, Network Evangelism, Relationship Evangelism, Discipleship Evangelism, Body Evangelism, Process Evangelism, Web Evangelism, Power Evangelism, Magnetic Evangelism.

Although the author argues there is no single method for reaching the world for Christ and recognizes the above methods as valid, he believes the only real method ordained by God is "people" – ordinary Christians ministering through the local church – Lay Evangelism. All other methods serve only as tools to support people.

[3] Wagner, C. Peter, *Eternity* Magazine, September 1977, offering evaluation of "Here's Life America" program.

[4] Barna, George, *The Frog in the Kettle* (Regal Books, Ventura, California: 1990), Page 227.

[5] For years Confrontational Evangelism proponents have taught that the Commission is given to the individual while Lifestyle Evangelism has taught that it is given to the church. But the reality of it is that the Confrontationalists are preaching it while the Lifestyle people are practicing it.

[6] Wagner, C. Peter, *Your Spiritual Gifts Can Help Your Church Grow* (Regal Books, Glendale: 1979), Page 177.

[7] My arguments against everyone being confrontational may lead you to believe you do not need to verbalize. On the contrary; although you do not need to be confrontational, you still need to verbalize your faith when the opportunities arise. I call this "non-confrontational sharing."

Strengths & Weaknesses of Dominant Philosophies

	Confrontational	Lifestyle	TEAM
Philosophy	Every Christian needs to present the Gospel A. Verbalization is mandated B. "Everybody" can learn how C. Doesn't acknowledge gifts	Every Christian needs to live the Gospel A. Verbalization is encouraged, but excuses are provided for not doing so B. Many can verbalize, but most are timid and cannot C. Acknowledges gifts	Some should be "evangelists" while all should be "witnesses" A. Some "must" (because of internal drive) verbalize B. Accepts the fact that most will never verbalize C. Is based on gifts
Personality needed	Based on dominant, outgoing personalities A. Confrontational	Recognizes different personalities A. Relational	Recognizes few are outgoing while *most* are timid A. Utilizes both at their own level
Communication method	Preset agenda with canned presentation	Flexible agenda	Promotes sharing through natural communication
Relationship to local church	Local church at center of activity A. Structured, highly organized system with leadership and controls	Not local church centered A. Leaves laity to fulfill Commission independent of others	Revolves around local church team A. Organized system puts local church at heart of implementation
Objective	Get a commitment A. Decisions without getting people churched B. Now or never	Make a disciple A. Network through side door B. Present the Gospel at earliest point of receptivity	Get them churched A. Getting churched is primary; getting decision is secondary B. Stair-steps prospects
Training provided	Provides how-to training A. But people won't attend (fear) B. Attempts to change personalities C. Structured for accountability	Encourages fellowship A. Limited "how-to" B. Attempts to make spirituality a prerequisite C. No accountability	No training required A. Only a simple understanding of the principles and an explanation of the application is needed B. Uses people where they are C. Accountable to leadership and to church as a team
Vehicle for carrying out application	Organized visitation	The individual believer	Structured system to organize laity to apply principles & laws (*TEAM Mate*)

	Confrontational	Lifestyle	*TEAM*
Identifying prospects	Everyone is a prospect A. Strangers: least receptive B. Develop relationship after decision	Develops prospects through building new relationships A. Acquaintances: mostly receptive B. Develops relationship while evangelizing	Identifies existing relationships A. Friends: most receptive B. Relationship already exists
Participants	Assumes all will fit	Freedom to be yourself	Utilizes the strengths of the individual
Method of motivation	Guilt	Concern for relationship	Holy Spirit through spiritual gift
Relationship to other methods	Rejects all other methods of personal evangelism	Conceived in reaction to and as an alternative to the misuses and abuses of Confrontational Evangelism	Accepts different methods as suitable for use with different people
Leadership	Trainees become trainers	Leadership participates the same as laity	Leadership leads, organizes, and administers while laity does outreach
Designed for	People with the gift of evangelism A. 10% B. Utilizes 10%; imposes on 100%	Laity A. 100% B. Utilizes members, but lack of structure leaves body unassembled	Fitting and utilizing both A. 10%/90% B. Utilizes everyone's gift as a team; thus assembling the body
Intensity	Intense continual pressure	Low-keyed	Low-keyed on an ongoing basis with short bursts of intense pressure
Spirituality	Assumes holy living	Promotes holy living	Recognizes the need for holy living

Chapter Two

REVIEW QUESTIONS

1. What are the four stages to developing an effective evangelism method?

2. What are some of the strengths and weaknesses of Confrontational Evangelism?

3. What are some of the strengths and weaknesses of Lifestyle Evangelism?

4. What are the strengths of *TEAM Evangelism?* How does *TEAM Evangelism* minimize the weaknesses of other methods?

DISCUSSION QUESTIONS

1. Have you previously believed there is only one right method of evangelism? Do you still agree? Why or why not?

2. Which method does your church use? How effective is it?

3. What methods are you familiar with? Which one best fits *your* personality?

Chapter 3

UNDERSTANDING THE TOOLS

To prepare ourselves for the *task,* we must not only understand the task and the method, but we must understand the tools we are to use to do the task. *Spiritual gifts are the tools given to us by God to carry out the Great Commission.*

Every Christian has at least one God-given spiritual gift to use in ministering to others through the local church. ("But every man hath his proper gift of God, one after this manner, and another after that," 1 Cor. 7:7.) Understanding your giftedness is the easiest way to understand yourself and God's calling on your life. In *TEAM Evangelism* each member plays an important role by using his own gift, thus allowing him to be himself. Therefore, knowing your spiritual gift becomes crucial if you are to fulfill your place on the team in carrying out the Great Commission.

Spiritual gifts are the tools for doing the work of the ministry. What is a tool? If God gives you a hammer, what does He want you to do? Dig holes, saw boards, lay cement block? No. Obviously, if He gives you a hammer, He wants you to drive nails. Determine what tool God has given you – what your dominant spiritual gift is – then you can determine your place on His team. You will then know where God wants you to serve. When you use the gift God has given you, you will receive *maximum fulfillment with a minimum of frustration.* You will work in harmony with other team members as they also use their God-given gifts.

Before you go any further in TEAM Evangelism, I strongly recommend that you stop and take the Spiritual Gifts Inventory (see Appendix 1 and the accompanying answer sheets) to discover or reaffirm your dominant spiritual gift as well as your secondary gifts. By doing so, you will get more out of this chapter and realize where you fit in the team.

Explanation of Gifts

Since the procedure of the Great Commission requires bringing an individual from a superficial awareness of God to become a mature Christian, a variety of gifts and a team effort is necessary. There are nine basic church-growth gifts that apply. A brief explanation of these gifts follows.

Evangelists have the Spirit-given capacity and desire to serve God by leading people beyond their own natural sphere of influence to the saving knowledge of Jesus Christ. *These aggressive soulwinners seek the lost.*

Prophets have the Spirit-given capacity and desire to serve God by proclaiming God's truth. *These hell-fire-brimstone preachers point out sin.*

Teachers have the Spirit-given capacity and desire to serve God by making clear the truth of the Word of God with accuracy and simplicity. *These scholars expound the doctrines and teachings of the Bible.*

Exhorters have the Spirit-given capacity and desire to serve God by motivating others to action, by urging them to pursue a course of conduct. *These "how-to" teachers give the application of God's Word.*

Pastor/shepherds have the spirit-given capacity and desire to serve God by overseeing, training, and caring for the needs of a group of Christians. *These leaders who feed their flocks and coach their teams are pastors, Sunday School teachers, and group leaders.*

Mercy-Showers have the Spirit-given capacity and desire to serve God by identifying with and comforting those who are in distress. *These comforters understand and uplift their fellow Christians.*

Servers have the Spirit-given capacity and desire to serve God by rendering practical help in both physical and spiritual matters. *These helping hands meet the practical needs of their fellow Christians and the church.*

Givers have the Spirit-given capacity and desire to serve God by giving their material resources, far beyond the tithe, to further the work of God. *These financial aides meet the financial needs of their fellow Christians and church ministries.*

Administrators have the Spirit-given capacity and desire to serve God by organizing, administering, promoting, and leading the various affairs of the church. *These take-chargers lead the church, its task groups (committees), and its ministries.*

Spiritual gifts represent the individual members of the body of Christ. There is a direct correlation between the various spiritual gifts within the church and the needs a church must meet in an individual's life to bring him or her to Christian maturity. I have developed a chart ("The Team Versus the Lost") that lists the needs on the left side and the gifts that predominantly minister to those particular needs on the right side. You will notice that the needs begin with salvation and work through the steps to Christian maturity. This chart helps individual members see how they fit into the team.

The chart and explanation is a reprint from *TEAM Ministry*. Its sole purpose is to show you a direct correlation between needs that God has placed in the lives of people and how He has equipped His church by working through a corporate body to meet these individual needs. Also, as previously addressed, in fulfillment of the Great Commission, we recognize that the Commission actually entails a variety of gifted people to carry it out. This chart shows you how God has equipped His team to take care of all of the needs in the body while at the same time using all of its members.

"The TEAM Versus the Lost"

Man Needs

God Provides

1 Salvation

2 the EVANGELISTS

3 Awareness of Sin

4 the PROPHETS

5 Doctrine

6 the TEACHERS

7 To Know How

8 the EXHORTERS

9 Shepherding

10 the PASTOR/SHEPHERD

11 Comforting

12 the MERCY SHOWERS

13 A Helping Hand

14 the SERVERS

15 Financial Aid

16 the GIVERS

17 Leadership

18 the ADMINISTRATORS

19 Fellowship

20 the ENTIRE BODY

21 to Serve His Fellow Man

22 A Mature Christian

23 the "TEAM"

24 "LASTING GROWTH"

Let's look at these needs one at a time and see how God has equipped the church to minister to them. (The numbering system will help you follow the chart.)

1 Salvation .... 2 the EVANGELISTS

Man's first need is (1) *salvation.* Romans 3:23 says, "For all have sinned, and come short of the glory of God." Who are the team members who meet this need in his life? (2) *Evangelists.* This is not to say evangelists are the only people in a church to lead others to a saving knowledge of Jesus Christ. But if you were to take a poll, you would see that evangelists are the ones who will probably reach 80 or 90 percent of them. (However, *TEAM Evangelism* can change that.) Evangelists are aggressive and confrontational salespeople for Christ.

What is meant by confrontational evangelists (called soulwinners by some)? They are the type of people who always try to motivate others to reach out to lost people. They are also the people who give testimonies like this: "I went on a trip and I sat next to a guy who wasn't saved. . . . As the plane touched down, the gentleman beside me bowed his head and accepted Christ as his Saviour." They can get on an elevator with a "sinner" on the sixth floor and get off on the twelfth floor with a "saint." Again, I need to stress that they are not the only people who can lead a person to Christ, but we must accept the fact that gifted evangelists are responsible for most of the decisions whether or not they are the ones who really influence the the people for Christ.

3 Awareness of Sin .... 4 the PROPHETS

Man's need to be (3) *made aware of sin.* Members who meet this need in his life are (4) *prophets.* They are people who can see what's wrong in other people's lives. They can see what's wrong in a church, although their ability to see everything that is right is limited. Their ministry is to point out sin. Prophets do what we think of as "real preaching" – getting excited, stepping on toes, and preaching for conviction, really stirring our conscience. These people are hell-fire-brimstone preachers.

5 Doctrine   6 the TEACHERS

Man needs to *(5) know the principles for right living,* in other words, *what is right.* People who meet this need in his life are *(6) teachers. Didasko* is the Greek word which means to teach: To communicate knowledge, to relay facts, or to make known.

7 To Know How   8 the EXHORTERS

Man needs to *(7) know "how."* Christians who meet that need are *(8) exhorters.* They spend much time teaching people how to do things. They also motivate people, challenging them to get more done.

9 Shepherding   10 the PASTOR/SHEPHERDS

Man needs *(9) to be cared for.* Through Scripture, people are referred to as sheep. We are the sheep and Christ is the Shepherd. If a sheep lays down with his head pointed downhill he can't get up or turn around without the shepherd's help. Who meets that need in his life? *(10) Pastor/shepherds.* Pastor/shepherds have the need to lead and to care for. They use the shepherd approach to leadership. They are burdened to teach the Word of God and to care for the people around them. They protect and shelter their flocks.

11 Comforting   12 the MERCY SHOWERS

Every person faces a time when he or she needs to be *(11) comforted.* Who meets that need? *(12) Mercy-showers.* They are soft-spoken, but outgoing people who seem to always know what to say when we hurt. When a tragedy happens in our life, who is the first person we call? Most likely someone with the gift of showing mercy. People with the gift of showing mercy tend to attract people who are either in the valleys or on the mountaintops of life. Mercy-showers help others face disease, death, loneliness, and other crises through their support and reminders that God is a loving God. They are also the first ones to send notes of congratulations and stand ready to celebrate the joys God gives as well.

13 A Helping Hand .... 14 the SERVERS

Sometimes Christians need *(13) a helping hand*. A family's car or roof may need repair and for whatever reason Dad cannot do it. A church building needs people who are willing to take care of the maintenance, spruce up the grounds and so on. A friend recuperating from surgery may need help with meals. *(14) Servers* receive great satisfaction from doing physical labor. This is a definite ministry that we need to promote today. It's a gift that God has given to many people in all churches. Servers are not kings but king makers.

15 Financial Aid .... 16 the GIVERS

Always existing is the need for *(15) financial aid*. Finances are needed to support the ministries and the missions in the church. *(16) Givers* meet financial needs and are very mission minded. It's not unusual to see a church that has several givers in it supporting many mission projects. These people enjoy giving to others who face financial burdens as well. This is another ministry that is drastically needed today. We should never belittle people who have this gift.

17 Leadership .... 18 the ADMINISTRATORS

The average church member needs *(17) leadership*. In order to reach a goal, 84 percent of the people in a church need a total program planned for them with constant supervision. If the program is laid out, 14 percent of them have the ability to meet that goal with little supervision. Man needs leadership because only 2 percent of the people have the ability to create a dream and carry it through to completion by themselves. *(18) Administrators* are the leaders.

19 Fellowship .... 20 the ENTIRE BODY

Man needs *(19) fellowship*. Who meets this need? The *(20) entire body*. All the administrators, the servers, the givers, the exhorters, the prophets, the teachers, the evangelists, the mercy-showers, and the pastor/shepherds. All these people combined together, the entire body, meet the fellowship need in a person's life. By the way, polls have shown that most people who start attending a certain church do so for the fellowship they enjoy. We go to church to be with our friends. In a big church a stranger has the tendency not to meet people and mix with people. It is hard to find new friends and a group with whom to fellowship. It is more difficult to meet the need of fellowship in a larger church, but it can and must be done.

21 to Serve His Fellow Man

In the center and reading from bottom to top of the chart is man's need *(21) to serve his fellow man.* I call this the catalyst need. Placed between the needs and the gifts, it ties together the whole concept of spiritual gifts and meeting needs. *Man needs to serve his fellow man.* God placed this need in the hearts of all men. People wrap their lives up in the lives of others. They don't have to be just Christians. Anywhere people are willing to wrap their lives up in the lives of other people, you'll see happier, more contented, and less troubled people – simply because they are meeting a God-given need. As Christians, we need to serve our fellow man by ministering through our spiritual gifts. In fact, we have a biblical mandate to do so. "As every man hath received the gift, even so minister the same one to another, as good stewards of the manifold grace of God" (1 Peter 4:10).

Cletis Garrett tells that "in over twenty two years in the educational ministry, I've never had a course responded to as well as the one I taught on spiritual gifts (using *TEAM Ministry*). The results have been tremendous. People are excited and involved. Discovering and understanding their own spiritual gifts, how those gifts work with other gifts, and where they can best minister motivates Christians to service. It has helped our nominating committee place potential workers and has helped others put their gifts into different places of service. We found out that Christians knowing and using their spiritual gifts really contributes to church growth, both spiritually and numerically. Serving in the place God wants them makes personal ministry interesting and exciting for church members. As a result, visitors and newcomers feel the sincerity and warmth of our members' concern in ministering to them. It draws people to our church."

22 A Mature Christian

(Back to the chart.) Let's add (as if this were a math problem) the left side of the chart. What do we get? *(22) A mature Christian.* After you have met all these needs in a person's life, that person becomes a mature Christian. Of course, if you don't meet all the needs in that life, this Christian won't become quite as mature. But, the closer we come to meeting all the needs, the more mature the individual becomes.

Tragically though, many churches miss one, two, three, or even all of the top four needs. To keep from making this mistake, we need to understand the *biblical procedure for training Christians*.

Second Timothy 3:16 states, "All Scripture is given by inspiration of God, and is profitable [for four things:] for doctrine, for reproof, for correction, for instruction in righteousness." We quote this Scripture very often to support the fact that we have an inerrant Bible. However, if we look one step further we will see a *biblical procedure* for training Christians. The procedure is first, doctrine; second, reproof; third, correction; and fourth, instruction. I don't think it is any accident that these four items appear in our Bible in this order.

Doctrine is the norms of the Scriptures. It teaches the standards by which we must govern our lives and our ministries. Doctrine is not the process of teaching, but the product of teaching. *Reproof* is to show what is wrong. *Correction* is to show what is right. *Instruction* is simply "how to" or practical application.

Notice the relationship in the chart. First, the ministry of the *prophet* is pointing out *what is wrong*, and the ministry of the *teacher* is pointing out *what is right*. The ministry of the *exhorter* is simply telling *how to do it*.

Some churches have a tendency to skip some of these people, and the person usually skipped is the prophet. After all, who wants a preacher stepping on their toes? The prophet makes us uncomfortable. In turn, we keep those who make us uncomfortable out of our lives.

Many churches lack a gifted teacher and a sound doctrinal foundation for their ministry. The person who is doctrine oriented is usually fact oriented rather than oriented to the practical application. But a good teacher, teaching theology, doctrine, and prophecy, week in and week out without giving practical application will have a frustrated congregation.

One of the most evident things lacking in meeting people's needs is simple, practical, "how-to" teaching. For instance, consider the man who says, "I know I'm a rotten father, and I know I do things wrong, but I'm tired of people telling me what I'm doing wrong. I want somebody to show me *how to* become a better father."

On the other hand, you cannot teach a man how to be a better father if you have not first convicted him that he needs to be a better father. Without conviction, practical teaching will go in one ear and out the other. At the same time, practical teachers cannot be effective if their teaching is not based on the sound doctrine and proper theology.

Sometimes we have teachers who can do both. Besides teaching, they have the gifts of prophecy and exhortation. But it usually works like this: Prophets get the people stirred up or convicted and practical teachers (exhorters) give the people the "how to," enabling them to change their lives. Teachers give them the doctrinal teaching and biblical facts that will prevent them from falling into sin again.

I want you to understand I am not talking about exclusiveness. Example: A man comes to you and requests help. You ask, "Are you saved?" He says, "No." So you say, "In that case, first, you need to go see Bob the Evangelist, so he can get you saved. Then you need to go across town and see John the Prophet so he can tell you what's wrong. Then come back up here to see Mary the Teacher so she can show you what's right. Finally go over to Jerry's house and let Jerry the Exhorter show you how to solve your problem."

No, I'm not talking about such exclusiveness, but I realize different people will excel in different areas of the ministry because of the varied gifts God has given them, even though a certain amount of overlap will always exist in all the areas.

23 the "TEAM"

(Back to the chart.) When the right side is added together, it totals *(23) the team. The team* is a group of active people indwelled and empowered by the Holy Spirit. No doubt about it, this is the most powerful force on this earth, and for years we have let this force lay mostly dormant. We have the most powerful force on earth, yet by doing nothing with it, we're letting the world and humanism and New Age take over our schools, our government . . . our families. As said by Edmund Burke, "All that is necessary for evil to triumph is for good men to do nothing."

24 "LASTING GROWTH"

The real bottom line for a church is *(24) lasting growth.* For lasting growth, the church has to meet *all* these needs in the members' lives. When you miss some of these needs, people are left incomplete and subconsciously look to fulfill the missing needs elsewhere. Sometimes after moving through several churches, they drop out completely, thinking that no church can meet their needs.

Let's be realistic, very few churches can minister effectively to all these needs. But, the more that are met, the more effective the church will be in lasting growth. Remember, growth does not come only when your needs are being ministered to, but growth also comes when you have an opportunity to minister to a need.

Balance – The Ultimate Goal

Some churches are strong on outreach. They are bringing people to Christ. At the same time people are going out the back door because the church doesn't have a good support program to back up their evangelism. Some have good teaching ministries, but don't evangelize. The whole idea is *balance*. The balanced church is a growing and effective church.

The Analogy of the Body

In all three passages where Paul writes on spiritual gifts (Romans 12, 1 Corinthians 12, and Ephesians 4), he uses a three-way analogy of the human body. The parts of the body are compared to the members of the church and the various spiritual gifts. First Corinthians 12 says, "For as the body is one, and hath many members, and all the members of that one body, being many, are one body: so also is Christ . . . For the body is not one member, but many. If the foot shall say, because I am not the hand, I am not of the body; is it therefore not of the body? . . . If the whole body were an eye, where were the hearing? If the whole were hearing, where were the smelling? But now hath God set the members every one of them in the body as it hath pleased Him . . . And the eye cannot say unto the hand, I have no need of thee: nor again the head to the feet, I have no need of thee. Nay, much more those members of the body, which seem to be more feeble are necessary."

Paul's analogy of the human body is an excellent example to explain this principle. For we can take the human body and chop off a hand – as a matter of fact you can chop off the whole arm – you can chop off both arms, both legs, both ears, and the nose, punch out the eyes, pull out the hair, knock out the teeth, and although the body is seriously handicapped, it does not cease to function. It just doesn't function efficiently.

The question is, *when does the body function most efficiently?* When it is all there; when every member is there and doing what it is supposed to do. The hands are being hands, the feet are being feet, the ears are being ears, and they are all working together for one common goal.

As team members use their gifts and contribute to the church's goal of meeting people's needs, they are blessed and fulfilled. As people's needs are met, they will become more mature and will be fulfilled. As everyone grows through this process, the church will also experience growth and excitement.

The Little Toe Principle

You might say, "I know that I'm part of the body, but I'm just the little toe. I'm really not needed. I'm not very important to the body, and I'm not effective at all."

I once knew a man who had his little toe cut off in an accident. The little toe has much to do with the balance of body. If you are the little toe in your church, you have the same effect on your church (the body of Christ) as this man's little toe had on his body. If you are the little toe in your church, you have much to do with the balance of your church.

The little toe really doesn't have any effective muscles in it. If you lean off balance, and start to fall, your little toe has no muscles to stop you from falling. But it immediately sends a signal to the brain that says, "out of balance." Then the brain sends a signal to a muscle in the right side of the foot to contract so your foot muscles can keep you from falling. My friend without a little toe had to pay great attention to what he was doing. If he ran, walked too fast, or if he wasn't paying attention, he'd lose his balance and fall. You may not even be the little toe, but you're still a very important part of the body. The worst thing you could do by being a little toe, is being a little toe that goes to sleep. The little toe that goes to sleep, just like the foot that goes to sleep, affects the whole body. You could be part of what's holding back your church.

In order to keep the team operating smoothly and effectively, every member must do his or her part. As the physical body functions best when all parts are properly working together, so does the church body function best when all members are active and doing their parts, working together as a team. The real bottom line of *team* work in the church is as stated in Ephesians 4:16, "From whom the whole body fitly joined together and compacted by that which every joint supplieth, according to the effectual working in the measure of every part, maketh increase of the body unto the edifying of itself in love."

In a Nutshell

God has uniquely equipped each individual with one or more spiritual gifts to perform a function in the body of Christ. "Now there are diversities of gifts, but the same Spirit. . . . But all these worketh that one and the selfsame Spirit, dividing to every man severally as he will" (1 Cor. 12:4, 11). Just as the physical body functions best when all parts are properly working, the church body functions best when every member is actively doing his or her part. The body of Christ is incomplete without all of its members using the gifts God has given them. The body will never be efficient or effective when all members are doing the same function.

TEAM *Evangelism* acknowledges that even though all Christians have a responsibility to be witnesses, only 10 percent have the gift of evangelism and are naturally aggressive and confrontational. The other 90 percent have equally important gifts that should be used in the evangelism process. Although these team members will not always be the ones who "close the deal" – who lead the person in praying to accept Christ – they all have important roles that contribute to leading that person to Christ. No one should feel compelled to perform a gift that God has given someone else, but everyone should exercise his or her own spiritual gift(s).

TEAM *MATE* INSTRUCTIONS

A brief discussion of spiritual gifts, our tools, begins on page 11 of TEAM *Mate*. Turn to page 15 to fill in the chart, "The Team Versus the Lost." This will help reinforce each member's place on the team. Take a spiritual gifts inventory to discover or reaffirm your own spiritual gift.

Once you have the results of this inventory, turn to TEAM *Mate* page 16 and fill in your dominant gift. Read the pledge on that page. If you agree to it, sign your name.

For a more detailed study on spiritual gifts, we urge you to obtain a copy of the author's book TEAM *Ministry*. TEAM *Ministry* explains the relationships of spiritual gifts to the local church, personal ministry, the will of God, the other gifts, and individual believers. Its unique approach to discovering, understanding, and implementing their God-given spiritual gifts helps believers find their best-suited area of ministry and become more effective and fulfilled in serving the Lord. The material stresses the importance of every member of the body of Christ becoming involved in the task of the Great Commission.

Chapter Three

REVIEW QUESTIONS

1. What must a Christian do in order to fulfill his or her place on the team?

2. What are the nine basic church-growth spiritual gifts? What are the results of team members using these God-given gifts?

3. What is the "Little Toe Principle"?

DISCUSSION QUESTIONS

1. What is your own dominant spiritual gift?

2. How does your gift fit into the team ministry?

3. What are some different ways to utilize your spiritual gift?

SECTION TWO

UNDERSTANDING
THE PRINCIPLES

Introduction

LEVELS OF COMMITMENT

In order for any church to do effective evangelism it is imperative that we recognize the existence of and identify two major groups of people in our churches: 1) people *with* the gift of evangelism and 2) people *without* the gift of evangelism. Those who do not have the gift of evangelism obviously have another gift. However, for the purpose of applying these principles to the function of evangelism, it is necessary to put the gift of evangelism in a group by itself while combining all others in a single group. The goal of *TEAM Evangelism* is to show those with the gift of evangelism how to incorporate their gift in an effective team while showing those without the gift of evangelism how to effectively reach out to those around them who need Christ.

In order to do this, we must recognize the difference between these two major groups and understand their relationship to the individual's commitment to Christ and the church. The following chart will help us do that. Keep in mind that it reflects commitment to Christ and the church as it relates to evangelism only.

COMMITMENT TO EVANGELISM
(The circle represents 100% of the church population.[1])

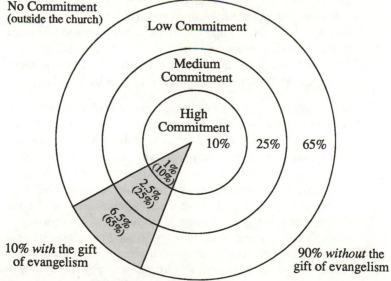

No Commitment
(outside the church)

Low Commitment

Medium Commitment

High Commitment 10%   25%   65%

1% (10%)

2.5% (25%)

6.5% (65%)

10% *with* the gift of evangelism

90% *without* the gift of evangelism

( ) percent of those with the gift of evangelism

Group One: People with the Dominant Gift of Evangelism

This group represents approximately 10 percent of the overall church population. Within this group are three types of Christians. (Because of their dominant gift, evangelism should be their primary area of ministry.)

1. *Those who have a very low commitment to Christ and the church.* They represent approximately 6.5 percent of the overall church population and 65 percent of those who have the gift of evangelism. Although they have the gift, their commitment to evangelism is no greater than any other Christian in the church. Their gift could revolutionize the church if they used it, but they don't. In many cases they are not even aware of their gift.

2. *Those who have the gift of evangelism and have a moderate commitment.* These Christians make up approximately 2.5 percent of the overall church population and 25 percent of those who have the gift of evangelism. When emphasis is placed on recruiting for visitation and outreach, these are the people we usually attract. Churches that have effective confrontational-type or visitation-type outreach programs have learned how to use these people effectively. However, when 100 percent of these people are utilized (which never happens) there is still only 3.5 percent (see below) of the overall church population doing evangelism. When it comes to sharing their faith, this group gives more testimonies and witnesses more than anyone else in the church. However, they are not very effective and do not get many results. If trained on how to work with *receptive* prospects, they could be very effective.

3. *Those who have the gift of evangelism and a high commitment to Christ and the church.* This group represents only 1 percent of the overall church population and 10 percent of those who have the gift of evangelism. Even though they represent the smallest group, they do 95 percent of all the personal evangelism that is being done. If it was not for this 1 percent, the church would have collapsed centuries ago. These individuals have a very strong burden to see the world evangelized and are willing to do whatever is necessary to accomplish this mission. In all honesty, *TEAM Evangelism* will not show this individual how he or she can be most effective. It does not teach how to get decisions, how to deal with objections, how to conduct a visit, etc., which is a comfort zone for those with the gift

of evangelism. However, I encourage everyone with the gift of evangelism to participate in TEAM *Evangelism* for two reasons: 1) TEAM *Evangelism's* strategy is to incorporate the gifted evangelist as a vital part of the overall church team. 2) Those with the gift will understand their relationship to people without the gift of evangelism and will show them how to work more effectively with these people. Otherwise this group finds itself imposing its methodology on the other. Even still, for those with the gift of evangelism, further training, beyond TEAM *Evangelism,* is advised. (Some recommendations are made in Chapter 8.)

Group two: People without the Gift of Evangelism

They represent 90 percent of the overall church population. There are also three levels of commitment within this group. (Because of their gifts, these people's primary area of ministry *should not* be evangelism. Very few should ever find themselves in the visitation program.[2] However, they still have the responsibility to be "witnesses"[3] while electing other areas, that complement their dominant gifts, for their primary ministries.)

1. *Those who have a very low commitment to Christ and the church.* This group makes up 65 percent of the overall population of the church. These Christians rarely get involved. Their attendance is irregular; their giving makes up only 10 percent of the overall budget, although their numbers represent 65 percent; and they get involved only when coerced, tricked, or pushed. This group will never suffer "burn-out" because their problem is "rust-out." They do very little if any evangelism, outreach, or witnessing in any shape or form. I will not address this group further, other than to say that TEAM *Evangelism* encourages these people and gets more of them involved than would have been otherwise.

2. *Those who have a moderate commitment to Christ and the church.* This group makes up 25 percent of the overall church population. They really care about people and want to do evangelism. They have a burden to see friends and loved ones saved. This type is also represented by two groups.
    Functionally backward or timid: When they are completely honest with themselves, they admit that they are afraid or really do not want to personally present the Gospel. Most do not see themselves as verbal, outgoing, or people oriented and avoid, at great

costs, putting themselves in situations that force them to be that way. They have a commitment to Christ and the church, but their barriers are larger. Efforts to get this group into any evangelism "program" or Thursday night visitation – or any training that is aimed at teaching them how to verbalize the Gospel – will continually fail. *TEAM Evangelism* works great for this group.

Outgoing: This second group contains those who see themselves as outgoing, expressive, and verbal. They would like to be able to verbalize their faith but don't know how. Yet, they still want absolutely nothing to do with organized visitation or outreach programs. *TEAM Evangelism* will get outstanding results with this group. If offered the right kind of training program, many of these people will attend. (Again, recommendations are made in Chapter 8.)

3. *Those who have a high commitment to Christ and the church.* This group makes up 10 percent of the overall church population. They are the faithful workers we have in every church. They will do anything they are asked to do – not because they want to or because they get fulfillment from it or because God wants them to, but because of their commitment. However, when it comes to evangelism, many in this group who are involved in visitation and confrontation find that 1) they shake in their shoes when they do it; 2) they respond only because of the guilt being put on them; 3) they get little or no results because of their ineffectiveness; and 4) they "burn out" on a regular basis.

The aim of *TEAM Evangelism* is to address the last two areas by:

1. Relieving the highly committed from serving out of guilt or simply duty and helping them recognize the dominant gift God has given them, thus enabling them to identify the area of ministry for which God has equipped them. Remember, when you use the gift God has given you, you will receive maximum fulfillment with a minimum of frustration.

2. Giving a suitable strategy to the moderately committed that allows them to reach out to those people around them with the message of Christ. After all, most of this group wants to do this. They have just been trying to do it in a manner that is not suited to them, a manner that does not fit their gifts and abilities.

Although I have said *TEAM Evangelism* is a method that fits 90 percent of the church (those without the gift of evangelism), I realize that no method, philosophy, or strategy will ever get 100 percent of the Christians involved in evangelism or any type of ministry.[4] Many agree with the findings of my chart on commitment. But instead of developing a strategy to *fit* the findings, they have attempted to *change* the chart to make it fit their strategy. However, results show that this group of moderately committed Christians (25% of the church population) will get involved when they are given a plan that will equip them to reach out while allowing them to be themselves. The remainder of this text explains the *principles* that make this possible.

FOOTNOTES

[1] The percentages represented here are considered averages. Many variables go into such calculations, for instance: 1) the age of a church. A new church will have a much higher level of commitment while an older church will have a much lower level. 2) A conservative church will have a stronger commitment than a liberal church. (Remember that we are talking about commitment in relationship to evangelism only.)

[2] *TEAM Evangelism* recognizes two types of visitation. 1) Shepherding: visiting like a Sunday School teacher or class leader would do. 2) Evangelism: visiting with the purpose of leading someone to Christ or getting a prospect to start attending your church. Just about anyone can do the first, while only a limited few can do the second with any success.

[3] The same as in a courtroom, a witness is one who, when asked, gives testimony of what he or she has seen and heard.

[4] This does not mean that the average Christian should not strengthen or increase his or her commitment; to the contrary, it is foundational to developing maturity in a person. However, witnessing should not be contingent on a person's particular level of commitment. History has proven that this does not work. Everyone does not reach the same level of commitment or spirituality. No matter what the level, each one can still be an effective witness.

Chapter 4

THE PRINCIPLE OF THE EXTENDED CHURCH

Years ago I was in the sign business. My business was located next door to a new car agency. I became friends with the owner. Now and then we got together and chatted business. One day he said to me, "I need a salesman. Do you know anyone looking for a job?" I replied, "I know someone, but I don't know how good of a salesman he would make." He said, "I don't care. I'll take him anyway." I made a couple of phone calls and Frank hired Jack.

Several weeks later, Frank and I met for lunch. I walked into his office. He was on the phone. While he talked with his customer, I wandered around his office looking at the things on the wall. I noticed a sales chart for the previous month. It read: "Frank, 18; Bob, 21; Joe, 13; Jack, 36." To my surprise, Jack appeared to be a much better salesman than I had thought.

When Frank got off the phone, in casual conversation I asked him, "Well, how is Jack doing?" He replied, "Not too bad;" to which I immediately replied, "Not too bad! He's already sold twice as many cars this month as you have! How can you say, 'Not too bad'?" Frank said, "Wait until next month." I asked, "Why? What's going to happen next month?" Frank answered, "Next month he runs out of friends and relatives."

Frank went on to explain that hiring salespeople like Jack is a very common practice for businesses that sell large ticket items such as appliances, automobiles, home repairs, etc. He also explained that most of these businesses have two types of salespeople. One is the person who is a professional salesperson. He is the person who has the reputation for selling refrigerators to Eskimos. These salespeople usually stay with the organizations a long time because they know how to sell and continually write orders. The second type of salesperson is just like Jack. They really cannot sell, but bring with them a whole new string of prospects – friends, neighbors, and relatives. The job turnover on the second type of salesperson is very high, but acceptable to all of the organizations because with each new salesperson comes a totally new group of *good* prospects.

The second salesperson is used to bring in the prospects, but in most cases the professionals actually do the selling. Frank went on to say that Jack did not sell most of those cars, he just brought in the prospects. One of the other salesmen did the actual selling because Jack really did not have the experience or ability to sell.

Friends and Relatives, Our Sphere of Influence

The same principle is true in the presentation of the Gospel. Most people in the church do not have the ability or the gift to clearly present the Gospel and to *get a decision*. However, everyone in the church has natural relationships – friends, neighbors, and relatives (personal prospects: receptive individuals) who need to be saved. In other words, these people are our *sphere of influence* (also called *circles of concerns* by some). The average Christian can work very comfortably within his or her own sphere of influence. George G. Hunter III writes, "The faith is not usually spread between strangers, but between persons who know and trust each other."[1] However, in our minds we always feel like we are being exhorted to work outside our limits when it comes to witnessing. Because of their outgoing personalities, gifted evangelists usually have much larger spheres of influence, plus they can comfortably work in or out of their sphere. The Christian without the gift of evangelism will be much more successful if he or she concentrates on the first and avoids the latter. On the other hand God has given the evangelist that gift for the purpose of easily confronting the lost person with the Gospel and asking for a decision. What I suggest is that we work these two together in the same sense as car salesmen work their two types of salespeople together.

What Influences People to Come to Church	
Advertisement	2%
Organized visitation	6%
Pastoral contact	6%
Invitation from friend or relative	86%

What influences people to come to church

The results of a national survey show that the following means influence people to salvation or joining a church: Advertisement (2%), Organized Visitation (6%), Pastoral Contact (6%), and Friends and Relatives (86%).[2] This reveals that the church will get the best results by reaching out to receptive people for their prospects rather than non-receptive who only become *suspects* (people who are so far out of our sphere of influence that we have little or no chance of influencing them). People we know and care about are the most receptive to us.

They are our friends, neighbors, families (parents, grandparents, brothers, sisters, children, aunts, uncles, cousins, in-laws, and so on), co-workers; people with whom we are familiar, with whom we have *existing relationships*. These existing relationships become our *personal prospects*. Suspects are strangers or people we hardly know. It stands to reason that since we care more about people we know and associate with regularly, then we will work harder to reach them for Christ. We have a stronger desire to see them saved and growing toward Christian maturity. This existing relationship makes it easier for us to get these people involved in our life, our church, and our Christ.

Westwood Baptist Church in Live Oak, Florida, used an attendance campaign in which members were responsible for inviting friends to church. The church's average attendance was 350. Their goal was 650. On the day they had set for their goal, the church had 830 in Sunday School and over 940 in worship. Pastor Sberna said, "The most exciting part is that we now have more prospects than we have had in the last three years. . . . Our people are absolutely overwhelmed by what we can accomplish for Christ."

New Life Presbyterian Church in Frenchtown, New Jersey, initiated an outreach and attendance program. Their regular attendance was 50. After much prayer and after inviting friends, relatives, and neighbors – their sphere of influence – the church had its "Friend Day."[3] There were 154 people in attendance (a 208% increase). Some of those friends invited were reported to have invited friends of their own. Two months later the church was still holding an average attendance of 75 (a 50 percent increase). Several people accepted Christ as Saviour as a result of "Friend Day." Almost one entire family accepted Christ.

Bill Slack, pastor of the church, states, "We need to realize, that in the cases of these conversions, the relationships that brought those folks to church were ones that had been cultivated over an extended period of time. They were also people who had been in our prayers for quite some time (in one case 5 years). The friends who came were friends indeed. They weren't just folks who were picked as targets. We cared about them, prayed for them, and pleaded with the Lord for their souls. I am convinced that a program such as this, based on existing relationships, will work in any situation."

Existing Relationships

Existing relationships are the key to growing the church. As I work with pastors across the country, I have found overwhelming evidence that churches that are actually growing are the churches that help their laypeople reach out to existing relationships. Existing relationships actually make up our sphere of influence. Stepping outside of our sphere of influence creates all kinds of problems for the average Christian. These same problems may exist for someone with the gift of evangelism, but the motivational drive that is given to them with their spiritual gift will help them overcome a lot of these barriers. People without the gift of evangelism will not have the motivation, desire or drive to overcome these barriers as they try to influence people outside their own sphere of influence. This is fine. However, most of us have been convinced either directly or by our own misinterpretations that the people we should reach for Christ are really those people outside our sphere of influence. George Barna writes, "One nationwide study conducted by Barna Research found that on any Sunday morning, one out of four unchurched people would willingly attend a church service if a friend would invite them to do so." [4]

The principle of existing relationships has not only been called our sphere of influence, but has also been called the principle of the *extended church*. The original research showed that the ordinary Christian has existing relationships with an average of nine people who are potential members of their church. Coupled with the fact that this research is several years old and knowing that this generation's social circles are shrinking, we believe that seven is a more accurate number for today. Therefore, *TEAM Evangelism* keys in on this principle by asking every Christian to commit themselves to identify, pray for, and direct their efforts to influence seven individuals to accept Christ and/or join their church. By concentrating on only seven personal prospects at a time rather than people outside of your sphere of influence, you will notice your results multiplying.

"But," you may say, "there are millions of lost people in the world. If each of us does not reach several people each month, we will never reach the world for Christ." *TEAM Evangelism* is not based on a few leading two or three people a week to Christ, but enabling everyone to reach two or three people for Christ in a lifetime, or at the most to set a goal of one person per year for every individual in your church. Doesn't sound like much, but if this were to happen, every church would double its membership yearly. Christianity would double every year, or at worst, if every individual only reached two people for Christ in his or her lifetime, Christianity would double every 60 years. And the best part is, these are realistic and obtainable goals.

As you identify these people and add them to your list, you may say to yourself, "I feel totally uncomfortable with trying to get these individuals saved." Or, "I would never be able to present the Gospel to these people." Don't be concerned with that at this point. Write their names down anyway. I have found, over the years, that many people avoid forming relationships with the idea of getting people saved because they fear the day when they will have to confront them with the Gospel. If you are one of those people, let me encourage you by reminding you that the goal of *TEAM Evangelism* is not for you to present the Gospel to someone. You may say, "I could never do that." If so, that's O.K. Plus, I'm not even going to trick you and try to get you to change your mind later. It is not necessary for you to make any commitment to present the Gospel to anyone yourself. But, (you knew a "but" was coming, didn't you) it *is necessary* that you make a commitment to pray for and reach out in a caring relationship to see that your friends will sometime, somewhere, have the Gospel presented to them. This is something anybody can do, regardless of how timid he or she may be. If nothing else, at the appropriate opportunity, offer them a cassette with a Gospel message on it.

Once you commit yourself to concentrating on the seven people whom you care about the most, you will find it much easier to do things with them that help influence them to take another step closer to accepting Christ.

Why people come to church

Surveys show that the number one reason people come to church is for fellowship. This fact stresses the necessity of building good relationships. *Event evangelism* (people coming to know Christ, establishing or strengthening relationships through sponsored or non-sponsored church events) involves building relationships. It is also an effective method for reaching those prospects desiring fellowship.

Reasons People Come to Church
1. To fellowship with friends
2. To bring children
3. To solve personal problems
4. To attend Sunday School
5. To study God's Word
6. To worship God

The Gift of Evangelism and TEAM Evangelism

The principle gained from the illustration about the car salesman at the beginning of this chapter offers an excellent example of how to utilize the gift of the evangelist.

Those with the gift of evangelism tend to be aggressive, confrontational, and in a true sense, sales-oriented people. They never have a problem stirring-up a conversation, breaking the ice or being able to get right to the point. But the key to the evangelist is that these things come naturally to him or her. In most cases, if you or I used the same tactics they use we would turn people off. Those with the gift of evangelism should be a part of an outreach, an evangelistic or visitation task group. TEAM Evangelism utilizes the evangelist in two major areas.

1. *Visit Visitors:* This group should follow up and visit people who visit the church without invitation from members. In other words, those who just happen to walk in to check out your church. They are also very effective in visiting nursing homes, prisons, newcomers to the community, etc. Many traditional books on personal evangelism will show the evangelist where to find prospects for visiting.

2. *Visit Prospects:* The evangelistic task group should be ready at all times to visit personal prospects at the request of team members. Sometimes a church member may have been praying and working with an individual, but for one reason or another does not feel comfortable presenting the Gospel to that person. However, they believe the individual is ready. Instead of letting the opportunity pass, they may request that someone from the evangelistic team visit the prospect. This allows the evangelists to spend most of their time with quality prospects who have been networked into the church by others on the team.

A point that needs to be stressed here is that the evangelistic team should not visit personal prospects without a request from the individuals who have the prospects on their lists. We need to be careful because sometimes we will find the same person on two or three people's prayer lists. One person may think the prospect requires a visit from the visitation team while another one does not. However, neither member is aware that the individual's name is on both lists. One person should oversee and coordinate church-initiated visitation.

Multilevel Networking, the Diminishing Prospect,
and the Unidentified Prospect

The principle of multilevel networking has been around in business for a number of years and has worked successfully for a number of products ranging from soap to automobiles. In recent years the principle has floated into the church and has been a very valid tool for gathering prospects.[5]

Although the principle has a variety of similar definitions, it works something like this: Just like Jack, in the previous illustration, everyone has a network of existing relationships around them. But unlike Jack, who was out of a job once the prospects in his network were sold, multilevel networking shows us how to gain additional prospects. Each one of the prospects also has a network of existing relationships around them and each one of their prospects has a network of existing relationships around them. As you can see, this could go on forever and ever. You can also see how rapidly it multiplies itself. If Jack had a network of seven people and each of those people had a network of seven people and each of those had a relationship with seven other people, virtually every new layer would be multiplying the previous level by seven. Therefore, the first networking level would be 7, the second 49, the third 343, the fourth 2,401, and so on. Sounds good doesn't it? But let's come back down to earth, because in reality it doesn't work quite like that.

Multilevel Networking

Jack's 7 Prospects		Each Prospect's Prospects				New Prospects	More Prospects
1	+	7	x	7=49	x	7=343	x...
1	+	7	x	7=49	x	7=343	x...
1	+	7	x	7=49	x	7=343	x...
1	+	7	x	7=49	x	7=343	x...
1	+	7	x	7=49	x	7=343	x...
1	+	7	x	7=49	x	7=343	x...
1	+	7	x	7=49	x	7=343	x...
Total 7	+	49	+	343	+	2,401	+...

Jack has 7 prospects. Each prospect has 7 new prospects. Each of the new prospects has 7 prospects, and so on. Prospects are multiplied as each new prospect brings in 7 more prospects.

Possibly the best illustration to show how it usually works is the chain letter. If you have ever observed someone who was involved in one and mailed a dollar to the first person on the list, then mailed letters to ten other people, you realize they did not get back the hundreds of dollars they were promised. At best they received five or ten dollars. It's the same principle. Regardless of our motives or sincerity the chain always gets broken.

I started off by pointing out objections with multilevel networking, but I still want to stress the importance of utilizing this principle in *TEAM Evangelism*. We must realize that it will not work as well as the dreamers say, but that multilevel networking brings something to your program that is needed – depth. The reason Jack eventually lost his job was lack of depth – he went no deeper than the network of his original relationships. This is why it is important to get new church members into the *TEAM Evangelism* system. With each new individual who comes in to your church, comes a whole new network of relationships and therefore a whole new group of prospects. The prospects from new members will give your program depth and keep it growing. Failure to do this will stop your program from growing because of our next principle.

Principle of the Diminishing Prospect

The Principle of the Diminishing Prospect simply states that the longer a person is a Christian the less prospects he or she has because there are less existing relationships within his or her sphere of influence who are not churched or saved. You might be thinking that we expelled this principle with presupposition number five in the beginning. The point being made there is that even though our circles of relationships do shrink, the person who has been a Christian for de-cades still has relationships with an average of seven unsaved or unchurched people. Newer Christians have even more. What we want to recognize here is that if we keep challenging the same people over and over trying to get them to reach the same people year in and year out, our efforts will become less effective. We need to:

1. As mentioned above, do *Multilevel Networking*. Work closely with and get all newcomers to the church involved for the purpose of meshing their networks into the outreach system of the church. Another motive for doing this is, if you do not pull their networks into the church, their networks are liable to pull them back out of the church.

2. Encourage existing church members to develop new relationships with non-Christians and unchurched people for the purpose of networking them into the church. Recognize that only a small percentage (those with the gift of evangelism, pastor/shepherd, mercyshower, etc.) will be able to effectively do this. It is important not to belittle the remainder of the people who are not able to perform in this manner. Get them involved in an effective area of ministry that allows them to use the gift that God has given them. However... (see next point)

Principle of the Unidentified Prospect

Now and then someone will argue, "I've been a Christian for years; all my relationships are in the church. I don't know seven unsaved or unchurched people." My experience has been that if you take the time to read through all the suggested names on the "Sphere of Influence" list provided on the following pages, you will be surprised to see how many names you are able to come up with. The list is designed to help you think. Thus, you will see how many unsaved and unchurched people you actually have around you.

How to Identify Your Sphere of Influence

The following list is to help stimulate your thinking, so you may formulate and prioritize a list of people whom you would most like to see become members of the family of God or of your church. As you go down the list, simply write in the names of people next to the descriptive term we have listed. Be honest with yourself. If it is someone that you really don't give a "hoot" about, don't list their name. Also, you may wonder, "I am not sure if this person is saved or not." Remember, our goal is not just to get people saved, but to fulfill the Great Commission. Therefore, if they are not attending church somewhere, write them down. I understand that you will not be able to come up with a name for every description, but list as many as you can.

My Personal Sphere of Influence

Person you care about	Name	Priority
Mother:	_____	_____
Father:	_____	_____
Husband:	_____	_____
Wife:	_____	_____
Son:	_____	_____
Son-in-law:	_____	_____
Daughter:	_____	_____
Daughter-in-law:	_____	_____
Sister:	_____	_____
	_____	_____
Brother:	_____	_____
	_____	_____
Cousin:	_____	_____
	_____	_____
Stepparent:	_____	_____
Brother-in-law:	_____	_____
	_____	_____
Sister-in-law:	_____	_____
	_____	_____
Mother-in-law:	_____	_____
Father-in-law:	_____	_____
Grandmother:	_____	_____
	_____	_____
Grandfather:	_____	_____
	_____	_____
Boyfriend:	_____	_____

Girlfriend: _____ _____

Niece: _____ _____

_____ _____

Nephew: _____ _____

_____ _____

Aunt: _____ _____

_____ _____

Uncle: _____ _____

_____ _____

Past Employer: _____ _____

Boss: _____ _____

Supervisor: _____ _____

Coworker: _____ _____

_____ _____

Work associate: _____ _____

Barber: _____ _____

Mailperson: _____ _____

Principal: _____ _____

Child's Teachers: _____ _____

_____ _____

Doctor: _____ _____

Dentist: _____ _____

Pharmacist: _____ _____

Optometrist: _____ _____

Chiropractor: _____ _____

P.T.A. Member: _____ _____

Beautician: _____ _____

Bowling Partner: _____ _____

Baseball Team: _____ _____

Volleyball Team:_____   _____

Football Team:_____   _____

Neighbor:_____   _____

_____   _____

_____   _____

Friend:_____   _____

_____   _____

_____   _____

Bridal Consult.: _____   _____

Wedding Party:_____   _____

Mechanic:_____   _____

Broker:_____   _____

Lawyer:_____   _____

Bank Teller:_____   _____

School friend:_____   _____

Business Person:_____   _____

_____   _____

Athletic Club:_____   _____

_____   _____

Political Groups:_____   _____

_____   _____

Union Member:_____   _____

Baby-sitter:_____   _____

Police Officer:_____   _____

Trade Assoc.: _____   _____

Garbage Coll.: _____   _____

Avon Lady:_____   _____

Other:_____   _____

_____   _____

Now you have listed the people you care about and have existing relationships with. This is your sphere of influence. Go back and prioritize them. This is not to say that any individual is more important than another in the eyes of God, but that realistically, in our eyes, some people are far more important to us than others. Take time to prioritize them on this sheet. (Read the *TEAM Mate* instructions that follow.)

In a Nutshell

Everyone in the church has friends, neighbors, and relatives who need to accept Christ. These people (personal prospects) with whom we have *existing relationships* are the most receptive to us whereas strangers (suspects) are often nonreceptive. Surveys show that 86 percent of those who attend church regularly, do so as a result of being invited or influenced by a friend or relative. Therefore, confronting strangers with the Gospel is not necessarily the only way to get results.

TEAM Evangelism shows you how to turn *existing relationships* into receptive and ultimately redemptive relationships to Christ.

TEAM MATE INSTRUCTIONS

Take the top seven names in your sphere of influence, prioritize them and enter them one page at a time in your *TEAM Mate* book, pages 24 through 36. This record will help keep you aware of your prospects' needs. To review the Principle of the Extended Church, read page 17 in *TEAM Mate*.

During the coming week, you need to make an intense effort to obtain all the personal information (spouse name, children's names, dates, etc.) on the seven people listed as your personal prospects. In the weeks following, watch for opportunities to gather additional information to complete your *TEAM Mate*.

FOOTNOTES

[1] C. Peter Wagner, Win Arn, Elmer Towns; *Church Growth: State of the Art* (Tyndale House Publishers, Inc.: 1986), Page 71.

[2] Based on surveys by Elmer Towns from 1984–1991 as part of *154 Steps...* seminars.

[3] *Friend Day*, by Elmer Towns, is a four-week evangelistic campaign that uses the principles taught in *TEAM Evangelism*. Over 40,000 churches have used *Friend Day* successfully. It is published by and available from Church Growth Institute, P.O. Box 4404, Lynchburg, VA 24502.

[4] George Barna, *The Frog in the Kettle* (Regal Books, Ventura, CA: 1990), Page 137.

[5] Business is given credit for developing multi-level networking. However, the process actually works better in the church than in a business, because, unlike the car salesman who loses regular contact with his prospect once he buys a car, the church actually strengthens the relationship by incorporating the prospect into the body, thus giving the church greater access to the next level of prospects.

Chapter Four

REVIEW QUESTIONS

1. Who are personal prospects? Who are suspects?

2. Why do most people go to church?

3. What is the Principle of the Unidentified Prospect?

DISCUSSION QUESTIONS

1. Who are some of your personal prospects? How many are you able to list?

2. What are the benefits of trying to reach prospects instead of suspects?

3. How can you work with the evangelist to get people to make a decision for Christ?

Chapter 5

THE PRINCIPLE OF PRAYER

Unquestionably, this was the hardest chapter for me to write in *TEAM Evangelism*. One side of me said to skip it completely, but the other side told me it's an absolute must, because *prayer* was a major factor in the success of the evangelism programs and campaigns I have been involved in through the years.

Even still, the more I studied and the more research I did, the harder it became to outline and formulate an approach. So finally, I decided to research what others had written on the subject. I pulled out all my books on evangelism and started looking for the chapters on prayer. Reasoning that if I could understand their approach, it would be easier for me to formulate my own. This is where I received a startling revelation – *no one had a chapter on prayer.*[1] In fact, most books on personal evangelism had very little to say about prayer. At best, many used what I call the "Salt-shaker principle." Their programs did not incorporate prayer as an actual part of the program, they just sprinkled a little prayer over it when it was finished. Prayer is *not* an "Oh, by the way" or something you sprinkle over the whole plan to give it flavor. *Prayer is a major integral part of any successful evangelism program.*

After seeing the neglect in this area I still decided to take a different approach. Although most evangelism books and programs do not address the necessity to and the "how to" pray, there have been numerous books written on that subject to help you.[2] Therefore, instead of "how to," I decided to examine the relationship of prayer and the prayer ministry to the overall evangelism program itself, looking at the areas which are seldom addressed and create the largest problems hindering the effectiveness of our prayers.

The Challenge

How does one *manage* a prayer program? *Most people will not participate in any kind of a group or public prayer.* When we print and distribute prayer lists only a few will volunteer to take them home. We can distribute the list to everyone and assign all to pray, but in reality we are only wasting paper. We can ask everyone to pray. They may indicate they are praying but how do we really know they are? How can we tell if they are praying and God is *not* answering or if they are *not* praying and therefore they are getting what they are praying for: nothing.

Four Types of Prayer

Functionally, there are four types of prayer – *private prayer, public prayer, individual prayer,* and *group prayer.* Understanding these four types of prayer and their relationship to all team members will show us how to get maximum results from our prayers, help us understand our prayers, and help us understand barriers that create major stumbling blocks in our efforts to get our team members to pray enough to make our program effective or worthwhile. Let's look at the four types, one at a time.

Private Prayer

Private prayer is defined as verbal or nonverbal prayer prayed within an individual's heart, home, or any private place. Have you ever prayed for someone to live – prayed for God to heal someone and extend their life? Could you list the names of everyone you have prayed for to live? Chances are you have forgotten 75 percent of them.

Have you ever prayed for someone to die? If so, you would probably have no problem naming of all these people. Why is that? I'm quite sure that if you have *sincerely* prayed for someone to die it was not someone you hated but someone you cared for very much. You came to the conclusion that the person would be better off if God took him or her home. The point I am trying to make is that when we pray for people we *really* care about, we pray more earnestly, sincerely, and more often, with greater discernment than when we pray for people we vaguely know.

For whom do we "really" pray? The bottom line is that our prayer time is dominated with prayers for *people we care about.* We may pray a simple prayer for someone in passing, but we are burdened for and pray often for those we care about the most. This includes our fellow church members as well as our personal prospects – friends, family, relatives, co-workers, neighbors, and so on.

I am convinced that the level of *sincerity* of prayer contains far more power than the words in prayer. It's what comes from the heart that really counts. Repeating prayers over and over or reading lists of unknown names without sincerity, in essence, all become "vain repetitions" if we don't really care.

God has given some people a *special ministry of prayer* (discussed under *Group Prayer*). We must recognize that this is a small percentage of the church. The average Christian does not have this special ministry. Although prayers for people outside our circles of concern can be effective when those people are friends of people within our circle of concern, we must acknowledge that as average Christians we are almost wasting our time when we read long lists and pray for people we do not know and for problems of which we are not aware. Not only are these prayers ineffective, but in most cases, the average Christian never really prays for the people on the list because they have no direct influence on his or her life.

I won't argue whether this is right or wrong, but I will suggest why some of these problems exist. We are bombarded today with people who have many different needs. On Sunday mornings we give our tithes and offerings (as we should), then a special collection is taken for someone who has financial needs in the community. We watch on television as helpless East African children starve to death. The phone rings; it's someone wanting us to buy tickets to take retarded children to the circus. We hear numerous pleas to get involved in helping resolve the drug problem. Pray for revival, stop drunk drivers, stop abortions – the list could go on and on. The more we are bombarded with the needs of others, the more insensitive we become to all the needs *that do not effect us personally.*

Therefore, it is imperative that we pray for people by *name AND need.* If it is true that average Christians pray only for those whom they really care about, then it is necessary for us to pray for them by name – not just a name, but a name with a face on it. Also, if we do not know why we are praying for them, our prayers most likely will be insincere and therefore ineffective. The key in making our prayers effective is being aware of those people around us whom we are willing to pray for and knowing the needs of those individuals.

James 5:16 tells us that *"The effectual fervent prayer of a righteous man availeth much."* Let's examine this verse. What is prayer? *Supplication:* a petition, appeal, or request. What is fervent? Earnest, sincere, zealous, eager, enthusiastic, to stretch. Who is a *righteous man?* A Christian, man or woman. We are made righteous through Christ. Finally, what is *availeth?* Effective, profitable, capable of producing results.

So when we petition God in sincerity and are willing to stretch ourselves in prayer for people, our prayers are capable of producing or getting results. Are there people around you whom you want to see get saved? Pray for them, *there is no better way to get involved in their lives* where God promises us the outcome.

Prayer is also God's way for Christians to get things done. He wants us to come to Him and ask, tell Him our desires, pour out our hearts to Him. "Ask, and ye shall receive" (John 16:24); "Ask, and it will be given to you" (Luke 11:9); "And whatever things you ask in prayer, believing, you will receive" (Matt. 21:22); "If you ask anything in my name, I will do it" (John 14:14). God wants us to acknowledge Him. When we go to Him in prayer, we are exercising our faith; we are showing God that we trust Him to listen and answer as He will. He promises that if we pray in His name, through faith, He will answer us.

Therefore, if we pray for our personal prospects to be saved, join the church, and grow to Christian maturity, God will answer us. Answered prayer is also a great testimony to prove God's power to those who do not believe.

What else happens when we pray? The Holy Spirit relieves our fear and gives us the desire and boldness we need to accomplish our task. Prayer builds our strength to stand firm on our convictions. "When they had *prayed,* the place was shaken where they were assembled together; and they were all filled with the Holy Ghost, and they spake the word of God with boldness" (Acts 4:31).

Public Prayer

Public prayer can be defined as praying aloud when there is more than one person present. I remember years ago listening to a well-known evangelist tell the story of his first public prayer. I'll call him Bill. He had only been saved several days when he went to lunch with his pastor and several other people. The food was put on the table. The pastor said, "Let's pray." When everyone's head was bowed, the pastor said, "Bill, you pray." Bill goes on to tell, "There I sat, a full-grown man, scared to death, turning numb, with no idea at all of what to say." Finally his mouth opened and the words started to come out, "God is great, God is good. Let us thank Him for our food... ." He said that when it was all over, "I was so proud."

You may have a similar story. Most Christians, at one time or another, have been called on to pray in public. You might have been like Bill. Although you were uncomfortable at the time, it gave you the strength and encouragement to eventually overcome your fear of praying in public. However, we need to understand that the fear of public speaking is at the top of the list of things all people fear. Someone once said, "The mind is a wonderful thing. It starts working the minute you're born and never stops until you get up to speak in public." The thing we must recognize is that public prayer is a form of public speaking. I have read nothing in the Scriptures that indicates this fear will automatically go away when we become Christians.

The point is, if we don't deal with this issue, prayer will become a threat and actually scare people away from our evangelistic efforts rather than add to their success. When inviting people to attend training sessions and orientation sessions on *TEAM Evangelism*, we should announce not only what we are going to do but what we are *not* going to do. Announce that, "If you attend, we are not going to call on you to pray or put you on the spot. We are not going to ask you to memorize Scripture and recite it back to the group. We are not going to ask you to read aloud." Promise them that we will do nothing to embarrass them.

Whether true or not, the average layperson *thinks* this is what will happen to them if they show up in any type of personal evangelism class.

The problem in dealing with fear is great because very few people will ever acknowledge that fear is the problem. They can come up with a multitude of excuses, change their priorities and accept a variety of abuses, but for a person who is suffering from this type of fear, the hardest thing to do is say, "I'm afraid."

Individual Prayer

For the purpose of *TEAM Evangelism*, individual prayer is defined as prayer by the individual participants or team members, either public or private, for those people within their sphere of influence. *Individual prayer* is where the real power of prayer lies in *TEAM Evangelism*. It utilizes the *principle of saturation* (addressed in chapter seven) by having people pray on a regular basis for those they care about most. By working with a prayer list and a prayer calendar (in the *TEAM Mate* booklet), individual prayer keeps you aware of the needs of those people around you. Prayer keeps you aware of the individuals to whom you have committed yourself to influence for Christ. It keeps you aware of what is happening in their lives. Prayer enables you to more efficiently relate to them by keeping you in touch with their needs and with God.

Incomplete Communication

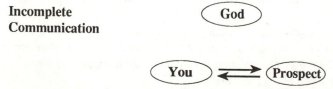

Notice the line of communication in the incomplete prayer triangle. Recognize how communication takes place without God or prayer in the picture. Communication is only between you and your personal prospect (two-way). However, in some cases it would be one way, because the personal prospect may not be receptive to you. Thus it becomes almost impossible for you to relate to his or her needs.

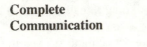 **Complete Communication**

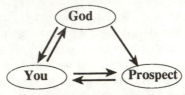

However, when God and prayer are put into the picture, the triangle is complete and new communication lines are put into place. Our illustration assumes that because your personal prospect is unchurched he or she is not saved. Based on Proverbs 15:29 ("The Lord is far from the wicked; but he heareth the prayer of the righteous.") and on John 9:31 ("Now we know that God heareth not sinners: but if any man be a worshiper of God, and doeth his will, him he heareth.") God is not required to hear the prayers of a non-Christian. But based on Acts 2:37-38 ("Now when they heard this, *they were pricked in their heart,* and said unto Peter and to the rest of the apostles, Man and brethren, what shall we do? Then Peter said unto them, Repent, and be baptized everyone of you in the name of Jesus Christ for the remission of sins.") God will convict the prospect of sin (rejection of Christ). God is aware of the prospect's needs and what is required to make him or her more receptive. Therefore, as you pray to God He can relate to areas in which you need to increase your sensitivity to minister to the prospect's need and strengthen your relationship. Notice that now you have increased your lines of communication with your personal prospect, you have five lines where without prayer you only had two or possibly one.

Staying aware of what is going on in the lives of the people we care about gives us the opportunity to put feet to our prayers. An age-old story illustrates this. In a Southern town there was a honky-tonk (bar and dance hall) that was a nuisance to the community and all law-abiding people.

One day a grandmother came to visit her grandchildren who lived near the honky-tonk. That evening at mealtime the grandmother suggested, "Let's pray that something will happen to the notorious place." They bowed their heads and prayed.

The next morning the children came running into their grandmother's room saying, "Our prayers were answered!" (The honky-tonk had burned to the ground that night.)

With a twinkle in her eyes, the grandmother said, "I know. I believe in putting feet to my prayers."

Though I do not condone any lawless act, I do want to stress that you must always *pray* as if everything were dependent on God and *work* as if everything were dependent on you. The *7 Touches* and *3 Hearings* (also discussed in chapter seven) are the feet to the prayers of the *TEAM* evangelist.

Group Prayer

For the purpose of *TEAM Evangelism*, group prayer is defined as a group of individuals who get together periodically to pray aloud or silently for the needs of the program, the leadership, the church, their team members, and their personal prospects. Every outreach program should have at least one *prayer task group* made up of people whom God equips for the *ministry* of prayer. Notice I did not say the *gift* of prayer. I believe that for the most part people attracted to this ministry have the gift of showing mercy. However, that does not mean that if you do not have that gift you do not belong or that all people with the gift of showing mercy should be in a prayer task group or that this is the only place to use that gift. The gift of showing mercy can manifest itself in many other areas. Some would argue that God gives a gift of *supplication.* I will not argue that doctrine other than to say, if you believe God has given you the *gift* of supplication or the *ministry* of prayer, you need to be a part of the prayer task group.

Unlike the average Christian, people given the ministry of prayer have a *sincerity* as great for the stranger as they do for a relative. Their prayers are never vain repetitions just because they have never heard of the person or have no idea what their needs are. They pray from their heart to God's heart regardless. Most have no problem praying publicly, but some may *prefer* to pray privately or silently.

In a small church, the prayer task groups will be involved in more than just the evangelism program – in essence they become a total church ministry prayer group. In larger churches, they can specialize on primarily praying for lists of prospects associated with their evangelistic efforts.

TEAM Evangelism uses these prayer warriors (those with the ministry of prayer) in two ways:

1. *Support the team and team members by praying for their personal prospects:* Lists for the needs of the program should be given to the leader to distribute to the individual members of the prayer task

group. Also, a list from every team member, including the member's name and the list of the seven personal prospects (from the TEAM Mate book) for whom he or she is praying, should be given to the individual members of the prayer task group. The members of the prayer task group will pray daily for these people on their lists. Also, the task group should have a regular meeting time to get together. Some groups may meet as often as once a week while others will meet only once a month. Several small groups may be more advisable over a single large group.

A note of warning: In the TEAM Evangelism program, the lists of names the members are giving to the prayer task group are for prayer only. The names will not to be given to the evangelistic task groups where they become prospects for visitation. Many members will not give names for prayer if they think someone is going to send a visitation team to visit them. The only time a visitation team should go visit prospects is when the prospects are uninvited visitors in the church or when a member has requested that the visitation team visit them. Confidentiality is a must in this area.

Members of the prayer task group should be warned against praying for the salvation of people by name in congregational meetings. If by chance the lost person is present in the meetings it can create a major barrier to their accepting Christ. Although we naturally think they should be glad that we are praying for them, it may be a matter of embarrassment to them and serve as a hindrance to their return.

2. Support special events with special prayer meetings: A second area where TEAM Evangelism utilizes the prayer task group is in an effort to intensify prayer during a period of evangelistic campaigns or high visibility events. During these campaigns or events, the prayer group should meet more often, a minimum of weekly, to pray for the needs of their team members and their personal prospects. During special events people should turn in names of prospects they have invited (the same confidentiality rule applies). The prayer task group will pray for them. Many prayer groups meet the evening before the event or campaign such as Friend Day for a late evening prayer meeting. In some cases all-night prayer meetings have been called. This has proven to bring great results by amplifying the efforts of the team members.

Once or twice a year have a TEAM Mate Prayer Day. Ask everyone to come and bring their TEAM Mate booklet. Pray for the progress of those listed in their pages.

Another caution to the members of the prayer task group is that because praying in public becomes so natural to them, they find it hard to understand those who do not want to pray in public. Many believe that those people only need some encouragement and if called on to pray two or three times the barriers will disappear. In many cases this is true, but in far more cases it may be very detrimental to the individual. I recommend that before you call on anyone to pray publicly, either be sure you have heard them pray publicly or ask their permission. Remember, you have probably only heard approximately 20 percent of your fellow team members pray in public. The question is, are the other 80 percent not praying publicly because they have not been called on or because they really don't want to? Always give them an out.

The Principle of Pay and Pray

The last item we need to discuss concerning prayer also comes in the form of a warning. I call it the *principle of pay and pray*. It goes something like this, "Well, you might not be able to do anything else, but you can always give," or in many other cases, "... you can always *pray*" (for our purpose, I will address only the *pray* part). In a sense, this attitude is the same as the one shown by the person who says, "I cannot do anything else in the church so I must have the gift of service." In reality, what they are doing is belittling the *gift of service* and saying it is of little importance. This is true when we say the same of giving or of prayer. By communicating prayer in this manner we are doing two things:

1. We are putting prayer at the bottom of the list and belittling prayer – saying it is not important.

2. We are allowing people to use our statement as a cop-out by not using the *real giftedness* of people. There is something that each of us can do using the gift God has given us *as well as pray*.

In a Nutshell

Nothing you can do will enhance the effectiveness of your evangelistic outreach more than encouraging and developing an ongoing prayer ministry that involves the individual team members and task groups. As we saturate our evangelistic efforts with prayer by name and need we go directly to God with the needs of the people we care about the most. In turn, God uses prayer as an avenue to show us how to minister to the needs that will ultimately lead those people to salvation and maturity in Christ.

TEAM Evangelism recognizes that there are two different types of people who pray. It keys in on both. Those who will sincerely pray only for their own prospects are given a practical system for organizing themselves to pray. Those who have a special ministry of prayer, and really desire to pray for many and much, are organized into task groups to pray for the needs of the program, leadership, team members, and their prospects. This structure provides overall efficiency for the program while minimizing the need to impose one group on the other.

TEAM MATE INSTRUCTIONS

Page 18 of *TEAM Mate* recaps the importance of prayer in reaching your personal prospects as you carry out the Great Commission. Read the pledge on page 19. Sign it if you agree to abide by it. Remember, it is a pledge between you and God only. Next turn to pages 24 thru 36 of *TEAM Mate*. Here you begin your record of seven personal prospects. There is a prayer checklist to remind you to pray daily for your personal prospects. Mark it off every day when you pray for those listed in your *TEAM Mate* book.

FOOTNOTES

[1] In all fairness to others, many authors who have written books on evangelism have also addressed prayer through other sources. In fact, John R. Rice felt that prayer was so important to the success of reaching people for Christ that he wrote an entire book on the subject. Billy Graham has developed specific prayer strategies in conjunction with his evangelistic crusades. Many other positive writings exist that are uncited here. The author's observation, however, is that no program or publication has developed a systematic and accountable program that incorporates prayer as an integral part of its evangelistic efforts.

[2] Books on prayer: *Abba Father: The Lord's Pattern for Prayer*, R. Kent Hughes (**Crossway Books, Wheaton, IL**). *Before You Say "Amen"*, Jill Briscoe; *Handle with Prayer*, Charles Stanley; *What Happens When Women Pray*, Evelyn Christenson (**Victor Books, a division of Scripture Press Publications, Wheaton, IL**). *Answering God: The Psalms As Tools For Prayer*, Eugene H. Peterson (**Zondervan Publishing House, Grand Rapids, MI**). *Too Busy Not to Pray*, Bill Hybels; *Jesus, Man of Prayer*, Margaret Magdalen (**InterVarsity Press, Downers Grove, IL**). *They Knew How to Pray*, Tom Carter; *The Complete Works of E.M. Bounds on Prayer*, E.M. Bounds (**Baker Book House, Grand Rapids, MI**). *Answers to Prayer*, George Mueller; *How to Pray*, R.A. Torrey; *Prevailing Prayer*, D.L. Moody; *Power Through Prayer*, E.M. Bounds; *Jesus' Pattern of Prayer*, John MacArthur, Jr.; *Elements of True Prayer*, John MacArthur, Jr.; *The Disciples' Prayer*, John MacArthur, Jr.; *Prayer Power Unlimited*, J. Oswald Sanders; *Sense and Nonsense About Prayer*, Lehman Strauss; *Unleashing the Power of Prayer*, compiled by Vonette Bright and Ben Jennings; *The Prayer Factor*, Sammy Tippit; *A Layman Looks at the Lord's Prayer*, W. Phillip Keller (**Moody Press, Chicago, IL**). *Principles of Prayer*, Charles G. Finney; *Answers to Prayer*, Charles G. Finney; *The Ministry of Intercessory Prayer*, Andrew Murray; *The Believer's Secret of Intercession*, Andrew Murray; *The Believer's School of Prayer*, Andrew Murray; *The Believer's Prayer Life*, Andrew Murray; *Revival Praying*, Leonard Ravenhill (**Bethany House Publishers, Minneapolis, MN**).

Chapter Five

REVIEW QUESTIONS

1. Briefly describe the four types of prayer.

2. How does *TEAM Evangelism* use prayer warriors?

3. What is the Principle of Pay and Pray?

DISCUSSION QUESTIONS

1. For whom and what should you be praying?

2. Think of the many prayers you have directed to God. What are some of the answered prayers you remember? Were they for people in your sphere of influence?

3. Why do you think prayer is so important?

Chapter 6

THE PRINCIPLE OF STAIR-STEPPING

"My mother is where it all began," says Frank Landrey, a Gideon. "She did what God wanted her to do when she taught her little 5-year-old boy a prayer. The prayer went like this: 'Now I lay me down to sleep, I pray the Lord my soul to keep. If I should die before I wake, I pray the Lord my soul to take.' Now granted, I didn't get saved through that prayer, but it was one step toward God that I needed to make. It was a beginning.

"I had another step toward God in my life; a step ordered by a man who happened to be a doctor and a Gideon. I didn't know what a Gideon was. All I knew was that he was a grown man and came to me, a high school student, a rising star in athletics – with some 50 scholarships available – who didn't have time for God. This dear man asked me to go to my first prayer breakfast. I said, 'Doc. I just don't have time. I'm so busy.'

"That grown man began to cry. I had never seen anything like that in my life. He said, 'Frank. You've just got to go. You've just got to go.'

"I replied, 'Doc, I'll go. I didn't know it was that important.' I went that next morning. I didn't get saved, but I heard the Gospel message. It wasn't until I was saved, that I realized he had done what God wanted him to do. Psalm 126:6, 'He that goeth forth and weepeth, bearing precious seed, shall doubtless come again rejoicing, bringing his sheaves with him.' And he brought me that morning.

"I took another step toward God when circumstances and my wife lead me. My wife's mother and my father died within the same month. My wife was saved as a young girl, but very shallow as a Christian. When our parents died, my wife went back to church. I went to the only fellowship I knew, the local taverns, and dove into the bottle.

"Soon afterwards, at the age of 28, I went with my wife to church – but only because of the leverage she used. Her leverage was that if I did something really bad – drinking, gambling – she wouldn't bring me home and air me out. She would just say, 'You owe me a Sunday.' So I went to church with her. I sat in the back, on the last of the overflow room, in the last seat, next to the door, so that as soon as the service was over, I could slip out. My wife did what God wanted her to do. She got me in the local church. I heard the Gospel there. There was conviction coming in my life.

"I went another step forward in an eye doctor's office at about the age of 30. In that doctor's office, God had a dear gray-haired lady who was working part-time, not just to supplement her income but as a mission field. She did what God wanted her to do. She witnessed to me. She said some words to me that changed my life forever.

"That morning my wife told me to say hello to Bertha for her. I didn't know Bertha. But when I walked in the doctor's office, she made her presence known to me. She said, 'Hello Frank,' with a beautiful, radiant smile. I said, 'Hello. Are you Bertha?' She said,'Yes.' I said, 'Carol said to say hello.' She said, 'Well that's wonderful, but Frank, are you sick?'

"I looked bad. I guess I looked real bad. There were some people sitting there in the waiting room. What was I going to say? I was pretty quick and said, 'Well you know when you have that great night the night before, the next day you pay for it.' They kind of chuckled. Bertha didn't say anything. She just turned around and went back to her seat at the desk, and waited her turn. When my name was called, she motioned me over. I walked over to where she was sitting and she motioned down. I thought, This dear lady can't hear very well. So I leaned over and looked her right in the eyes. She looked at me with all the love that she could muster and whispered, 'Frank, if you would trust Jesus, you would never have to be drunk again.'

"I went straight up. It was like she hit me with a two-by-four. Her words were so powerful. I did not know what to say. I stood there for a moment or two and I'm afraid I shook visibly. Then I went on into the doctor's office. I was mad, but I couldn't say anything back, because I realized that this lady loved me. She was not trying to make a show of herself, because I realized she could have said that out loud to me right in front of all my peers. But you see, she wanted me and me alone. I later found out that she biblically 'spoke the truth in love.'

"Finally, there was a pastor in my life who did what God wanted him to do. I'd come home from work and was very tired. My wife spoke up, 'I got a phone call today. The pastor called and he is coming over.' I said, 'He is, huh. He's coming over?' She said, 'Yes he is.' I said, 'Well I'm going to do exactly what I always do. I'm not going to be any different.'

"When the pastor came in, he said, 'Frank, I've come because some people have asked me to come. I'm new at the church and I just wanted to visit you and share some things with you.' We hadn't talked for three minutes when I said, 'Excuse me. I have got to go do something that I normally do at night. I know you won't mind.' I got a beer out of the refrigerator, popped it, and began to drink it.

"That man did what God wanted him to do. He didn't attack the error in my life, as every other preacher had done. Others had argued with me over whether you should or shouldn't drink and lost the whole concept of being saved. That pastor began to share with me that I was a sinner, that he was a sinner, and that the only difference between us was that he was a saved sinner and I was a lost sinner. I knew I was a sinner. He began to share how Jesus came and lived and died for my sins. He shed His blood for my sins. And that only in Him could I find the open door. Only in Him could I find eternal life. Peace. And oh Lord, how I needed peace. I was doing well on the outside, but I was so empty on the inside. So I heard him loud and clear, but I acted like I didn't.

"As he got ready to leave, he said, 'Are you ready, Frank?' I said, 'No.' He said, 'I want to tell you something, that if you quit your drinking, you will not be ready; for it's not quitting drinking that gets you ready, it's with the heart man believes unto righteousness. God wants your heart Frank. He doesn't want your works. Now if you do the works because He's got your heart, that's different.'

"Powerful words. I couldn't sleep that night.

"Finally, on Sunday, December 27, 1970, in a church pew, I realized that I needed and wanted a Saviour."

The Stair-Stepping Process

The process that led Frank Landrey to Christ is called stair-stepping. Different people at different times, did what God wanted them to do, to bring him one more step closer to accepting Christ. Stair-stepping is a term that was originated by Dr. Elmer Towns to denote the steps that an individual goes through as he or she grows toward Christian maturity. The concept of stair-stepping also fits the process of the Great Commission and ties together the process of evangelism with spiritual gifts. It involves church members and their gifts in a variety of steps a person climbs in the process of going from having a superficial awareness of God, to becoming a mature, Christlike person. Stair-stepping provides divisions for the steps and titles them, thus giving us a clearer indication of what we need to do to get an individual from one step to the next step. Also, clear division of these steps shows us that different steps are different functions and therefore require diverse types of people and gifts to minister to people at these various levels of maturity.

The story of Frank Landrey shows how powerful stair-stepping can be, even when it is unplanned, unorganized, and stretched over a long period of time. This chapter will show you how to make stair-stepping far more effective by utilizing this principle in a systematic plan.

When you stair-step people toward the Gospel, it is not necessary to confront them with a "now-or-never" decision. If you do this and the prospects do not accept Christ, they may be left feeling that they have turned their backs on God. The door of opportunity begins to close and the unsaved are farther away from God than before they were pressed with the "now-or-never" decision. In stair-stepping you gently help people walk toward God in an inoffensive manner. Always leave an open door.[1] Recognize that the Gospel itself may be very offensive to those rejecting it. Your goal is not to let them reject it because of your presentation.

First you must recognize the unchurched or lost and begin to use your relationship to draw them up the steps. As you begin to cultivate the relationships and invite prospects to events, the prospects become more receptive. Before long they accept your invitation. You do not need to press them for a salvation decision at home. Let them go to church and hear the Gospel or attend events[2] where the opportunity may arise to present the Gospel to them. Somewhere along the line, whether before or after (probably after) they attend church, the prospects will get saved. Your goal is to reach them, instruct them, get them in church, lead them to Christ and get them to actively participate in a local church, then teach and nurture them into being mature, "Christlike" Christians.

Stair-stepping can begin at any of the various steps in the process, depending on where the individual is to start. Some may come from a heathen background while others come from a Christian home. Although your ultimate goal is to see your personal prospects become mature Christians, the most important step in that process is to see them reach a point of salvation – to "get saved" (accept Christ, become born-again, adopt the Christian faith). Stair-stepping cannot be complete without the salvation of your personal prospects. Therefore, your plan should be to communicate the Gospel (or see that it is communicated) at the earliest point of receptivity.

If the people you have keyed as personal prospects do not go to church but say they are saved, do not drop them. (Remember the goal is to develop mature Christians.) This means they just start on the stair-stepping scale at different points.

The Stair-Stepping Scale

There are various opinions as to the number of items that should be on a stair-step. Plus there are a number of stair-stepping charts in print. However, they are all a variation of or adopted from what the Church Growth Movement has termed the "Engel's Scale."[3] The following list shows the typical stair-steps a prospect climbs. It reads from bottom to top.

POST-CONVERSION	16.	Becomes Christlike.
	15.	Observes regular personal devotions and prayer.
	14.	Uses his/her spiritual gifts in local church ministry.
	13.	Personal finances are based on biblical stewardship.
	12.	Accepts and is working toward God's design for the family and home.
	11.	Actively shares his/her faith.
	10.	Participates in discipleship training.
	9.	Faithfully participates in church worship, study groups, or Sunday School.
	8.	Publicly acknowledges faith/conversion (in church or among friends).
S	S.	Salvation/conversion experience. Accepts Christ as Saviour. Adopted into the family.
PRE-CONVERSION	7.	Is willing to repent and accept Christ.
	6.	Realizes sin keeps him/her from salvation.
	5.	Recognizes that Christ is the bridge to God and his/her salvation.
	4.	Realizes he/she is a sinner.
	3.	Believes he/she is responsible to God.
	2.	Has faith that there is a supreme being.
	1.	Has only a superficial awareness of God.

We recognize that no one will fit this list exactly as laid out. Many items may be rearranged to fit many individuals. Plus, we have placed recognition of salvation between 7 and 8, which could truly come earlier or later. That is why it is identified with an "S" instead of a number.

Salvation: A Process Leading to an Event

Why would I say that salvation does not come at a recognizable point for everyone? Over the years I have found it interesting to hear the testimonies when a group of Christians get together. I have one friend who begins his testimony talking about a man he was witnessing to. The man trying to redirect the conversation, questioned him, "You don't really think that Jesus turned water into wine do you?"

He replied, "Well, I really don't know if Jesus turned the water into wine because I wasn't there. But, if you'll come over to my house, I'll show you where Jesus turned wine into furniture, clothing, food, and a caring husband and father."

This man was the town drunk. He literally knew what it was like to sleep in the gutter. When he accepted Christ, he got what we call *SAVED*. He immediately got rid of the obvious sin areas in his life. He went home and did some "house cleaning." The following week he got a job and has worked every day since. Today he is chairman of the deacons in his church. (His changes did not get him saved, but they were an outward expression of his salvation.)

This is what we call the "Road-to-Damascus"[4] experience. Usually when such a testimony is given, one or two other Christians in the group will give a similar testimony. Their testimonies fit what I have heard so many preachers and evangelists say, "If you do not know the day, the hour, and the minute you got saved, you need to get saved."

I started doing something different when I heard people giving these types of testimonies. I started giving my own testimony which went something like this, "You know, I didn't get saved like that. I really don't know the day, the hour, or the minute that I got saved. In 1954, as a child, I supposedly confessed Christ as my Saviour (being raised in the church, I knew all the right answers). However, as I look back, I know I was not saved at that time. In fact, I am sure that I got saved somewhere between 1969 and 1970. I really can't tell you the exact time. Yet, at the same time, I don't doubt for one second that I am saved."[5]

Here is the clincher, though. After hearing my testimony, a lot more people in the room felt more comfortable in giving their testimonies. Because we have been conditioned to listen to testimonies of the "Road-to-Damascus" type of experience, many people who do not have that type of testimony feel ashamed to give their own. Furthermore, many question their own salvation because they do not know the exact day, hour, or minute. In reality, most people relate to the latter. Once they fully understand the salvation experience, most realize they did not get saved when they first professed to have. You don't get saved when you simply *verbalize* a commitment to Christ. You get saved when you "confess with thy mouth (*verbalize*) the Lord Jesus, and shalt believe in thine heart (*have faith*) that God hath raised him from the dead," Romans 10:9 (*italics mine*). In reality, you get saved when the Holy Spirit *indwells* you. Let's face it, verbalization and indwelling do not always happen at the same time.

When a person gets saved, it is always an event, an event that has the angels in heaven rejoicing (Luke 15:10). But, in most cases, this event is not quite as earthshaking for us below. When a person walks along a line on one side and crosses to the other side, it is an event. However, unlike the person who runs and jumps six feet to get over the line, many of us walk alongside that line for miles and miles. One day we just notice that we are on the other side. We are not positive of when we crossed over, but we do know that we are on the other side. In fact, we were so close to the line that when we crossed over, it was such a small event, such a small step, that it was hard for us to recognize at that moment. I am *not* teaching *progressive salvation*. We must recognize that in many cases people go through a progressive acceptance or progressive awareness coming to the knowledge of their salvation experience.

If this is true, then do we want to help God by writing names in His *Lamb's Book of Life* every time someone responds to an invitation or is counseled? Is that individual saved simply by reciting the sinner's prayer? Or is he saved when he announces to the pastor or a friend that he wishes to accept Christ as his Saviour? Or was he possibly saved the week or month before – or after? For this reason, we need to recognize salvation as being a process leading up to an event and not merely an event.

The Importance of Networking

Many people will come into a church and announce publicly or privately that they accept Christ, but they really do not sincerely accept

Him. Often, through lack of interest or lack of bonding them to the church before the real event takes place, we allow them to get out of the church. George Hunter, III, writes, "Most of the people who became Methodist converts first joined a class, and sometime later *became* conscious Christians!"[6]

This is why it is so important to network people into the local church. If we let people drift in and out of our churches without true conversion, are we really helping the cause of Christ? This is where the rest of the team becomes involved. The support gifts, the gifts of service, exhortation, giving, teaching and so on, now minister to their needs and serve to bond new members to the local church whether they have truly accepted Christ in their hearts or not. *The odds of them coming to a true conversion is many times higher when they participate in the church than it would be with them sitting at home watching television.* This is why we put such great importance on enfolding people into your church.

In a Nutshell

Evangelism is not a now-or-never decision-making situation, but a process. It involves a variety of steps a person climbs in the process of going from having a superficial awareness of God, to becoming a mature, Christlike person. The process does not stop the moment a prospect receives Christ as Saviour or joins the church. It continues as team members minister to and teach the newcomer all the things the Bible has taught them.

In *TEAM Evangelism*, *TEAM* members lead prospects in an inoffensive manner to stair-step them toward salvation and Christian maturity.

TEAM MATE INSTRUCTIONS

Turn to pages 24 thru 36 of *TEAM Mate*. Here are the records of your seven personal prospects. At the bottom of the page is a place to note where you believe each personal prospect is in the stair-stepping process. Update your stair-step table as the individual grows. Use a pencil to mark it since you will need to update it periodically. This will help you keep up with the progress of each prospect.

FOOTNOTES

[1] "Now or Never" is not only a way to close the door for some people but also a way to get an insincere answer from others, as well as being a very offensive method to use. It is important that all methods we use are effective in bringing people to Christ and

leave everyone who rejects them unoffended and open to a Gospel presentation from someone else.

[2] I do not want you to think that all you have to do to get someone saved is just invite them to church. Someone once said to me, "Now I see how *TEAM Evangelism* works. You get people to invite others to church, where you get the pastor to preach them down the aisle. This means the laypeople are *inviters*." On the contrary. If inviters were all we needed we could hire them. Yes, we want you to invite them, but if you have not established, cultivated, and developed caring relationships (on both sides) you will only be wasting your time by inviting these people to church. Because if someone (it may be you or someone else) has not prepared the soil, the people are not going to "take root" anyway. Being a good *TEAM* Evangelist requires much more than being just an inviter.

[3] Engel, James E. and Norton, Wilbert, *What's Gone Wrong With the Harvest* (Zondervan),1975.

[4] The Road-to-Damascus denotes the dramatic salvation experience of Paul when he met Christ on the road to Damascus (Acts 9:3).

[5] Even though more Christians can relate to this type salvation experience, it leads most to deal with assurance of salvation later in life.

[6] George G. Hunter, III, unpublished manuscript on John Wesley's methods of evangelism.

Chapter Six

REVIEW QUESTIONS

1. What are the goals of stair-stepping?

2. Describe a "now-or-never" decision and tell why pressing for one may be wrong.

3. What is the "Road to Damascus" experience? Does everyone have one?

DISCUSSION QUESTIONS

1. As a group, team members should discuss their salvation experiences. Were members pressed for a "now-or-never" decision? Were they stair-stepped? Was the decision to accept Christ made at home or in church? Discuss the pros and cons of the ways they were lead to Christ.

2. Does the idea of stair-stepping someone to Christ make you more comfortable with the thought of evangelism? Why? Are you more inclined to be involved in the process?

3. Are your personal prospects at various levels in the stair-stepping process? What are some ways you can help stair-step these people to Christian maturity?

Chapter 7

THE PRINCIPLE OF BONDING

Think through a hypothetical situation with me for a moment. Many of you, at one time or another, have been involved in or know someone in some type of sales, whether it be selling magazines, encyclopedias, or vacuum cleaners. If you did not sell something door to door yourself there's a good chance you bought something from a door-to-door salesperson.

Imagine you were on the road for a week and sold ten sets of encyclopedias. At the end of the week, you returned to your office, gave the ten orders to your secretary and told her, "Mrs. Jones, before you ship these orders, will you call all ten of these people and say, 'Our salesman was in your home this week and sold you a set of encyclopedias. Before we ship them, we would like to give you an opportunity to cancel the order. If you really don't want the encyclopedias, we will tear up the order at this moment and you will never hear from us again. Would you like your encyclopedias shipped?" The question is, out of the ten orders you started with, how many would you still have after the phone calls were made? Now and then I ask that question to an overzealous salesperson who will say, "Well, at least nine." However, most people are realistic enough to say, "We would be lucky if we had three."

Why is it that we would lose so many orders by giving the people an opportunity to cancel? Because the people never *bought* these encyclopedias to start with. They were *sold* encyclopedias. How many items do you own that you never *bought* but had *sold* to you?

The whole point I am trying to make is that when it comes to the Gospel, it must be bought; it can never be sold. That means that a simple emotional "yes" or a "yes" to get the "salesperson" out of their house did not get an individual saved. However, the salesperson might have that individual thinking he is saved, which can do more harm than good. There is often a great gap between "getting a decision" and "making a Christian." The answer is not just to get a decision, but to do what is necessary to get the individual regularly attending a local church.

This process is called bonding (also called assimilation). Bonding (a term popularized by Elmer Towns) is getting people to stick to the church. Towns writes, "Relationships are the glue that bonds people to the church."[1]

Much material written on Lifestyle, Relationship, and Network Evangelism put great importance on establishing and strengthening relationships in order to network people into the church and bond them into a group. However, much of the material leaves us believing we are to deal only with strangers. It seems as if Christians have made a pact, "You reach my friends and I'll reach your friends," thus leaving us all to reach out to strangers. Because *TEAM Evangelism* starts with existing relationships, the hardest step in bonding has already been taken.

The principle of bonding says we must get new people involved in groups or they will not stay in the church. Easily stated: The fewer relationships one has within the church, the more apt that individual is to leave; the **more** relationships a newcomer has within the church the greater his potential of staying. Bonding increases the strength of the relationship to the church. O.J. Bryson, in his book Networking the Kingdom, calls it, "The Rule of Seven: When a church member has seven close friends in a church, he or she will never leave it."[2]

Elmer Towns writes, "A new convert must become a part of a primary group within the church within two weeks of joining the church or he will become a dropout statistic. The new convert must do more than join the local church, he must become identified with a sub-group within the church."[3] Therefore, bonding is most effective when it is done before the person starts becoming active in the church. If it has not been done beforehand, the first several months become crucial. Charles Arn offers the following chart to support the idea that the number of friends a person makes during the first six months of their church life directly influences whether that person continues as an active member or drops out. It compares 100 people; 50 active and 50 inactive.[4]

Number of New Friends in the Church	0	1	2	3	4	5	6	7	8	9+	Totals
Active	0	0	0	1	2	2	8	13	12	12	50
Drop-outs	8	13	14	8	4	2	1	0	0	0	50

However, if getting people to accept Christ and join the church were as easy as having an existing relationship, our churches would be overflowing. We all have relationships with people who want nothing to do with our "religion." Therefore, we must realize that what is needed is a three-way relationship, not just a single relationship. First is their relationship with you, second is their relationship with your church (its members), and third is their relationship to Christ. In order to reach someone for Christ, you must first *win them to you,* second *win them to your church,* then and only then can you *win them to Christ.* If they reject you or your church they will reject Christ.

Luke 10:16 states, "He that heareth you heareth me; and he that despiseth you despiseth me. . . ." Winning them to you will be easier because by dealing with people with whom you have existing relationships, in most cases, they have already been won to you. Therefore, the task ahead of you is to play a role in establishing and developing the last two relationships. Drs. Win and Charles Arn, in *The Master's Plan for Making Disciples,* write, "Every opportunity for non-Christians to rub shoulders with church members provides an additional personification of Christ's love."[5]

A prospect will become much more receptive to the Gospel as relationships are developed and strengthened. If we plan for the individual to hear a presentation of the Gospel at their *earliest point of receptivity,* then we need to stress that activities that present the Gospel should not be the first thing to try to get unsaved people to participate in. Remember a presentation of the Gospel asks for a commitment to Christ and in all cases the *acceptance of a whole new value system for their life.* This means that some are not taking the next step, but five or six steps at once. Individuals will be much more receptive to making this commitment if they have established a trusting relationship with you and the church and understand this value system. This is best done through *The 7 Touches* and *The 3 Hearings.*

The 7 Touches and The 3 Hearings

As discussed in chapter 5, prayer is possibly the most powerful tool we have available to use to do effective evangelism. However, if all we do is pray, our outreach will be ineffective. As stated earlier, you must always *pray* as if everything were dependent on God and *work* as if everything depended on you. Prayer needs hands and feet. *The 7 Touches* and *The 3 Hearings* are the hands and feet of TEAM Evangelism.

The 7 Touches

Introducing *The Law of the 7 Touches,* Towns writes, "Research shows that a person usually makes a meaningful decision for Christ after the church has contacted him seven times." *The 7 Touches* are built on the *Principle of Saturation.*

The Principle of Saturation

This principle is best illustrated in advertising. As you watch television this evening you will see that same commercial repeated over and over and over until it almost becomes an irritant to you. Yet at the same time, advertisers could be paying as much as $800,000 per minute for these commercial spots. Why do they spend millions of dollars to irritate you? Because they are aware that repetition builds strength in the position of their product, builds awareness of their product, and in turn gives them the results they are looking for: sales and profits. Repetition builds saturation.

The principle of saturation recognizes that touching someone's life in any area only once will make little impact or influence on them. *The 7 Touches* draw people into relationships that show you care about the people in order to bond them to your church. You can use many of the items listed in *The 7 Touches* to help strengthen those relationships that are weak. The real challenge for you is not to put all of your emphasis on establishing and strengthening the relationships that already exist but to network the relationships with other people in your church. This can be done by a number of activities. Many of these activities should involve other church members besides yourself. This helps the individual establish relationships within the church, which are necessary if we are going to win them to the church and ultimately win them to Christ.

A Variety of Activities

A variety of activities may be used, not necessarily all church related. In fact, the smaller nonchurch-related activities can serve to establish relationships easier than the church-related activities which usually involve a large number of people. Unsaved people feel uneasy attending a function that includes a lot of people they don't know, especially if they are forced to interact. For that reason, if you use the tactic of inviting new prospects to large church functions only, you will find that in most cases, the answer you will get is "No." Take time to develop relationships. You don't need to push them to make a decision today. If the person is 20 years old the odds are only 1 in 200,000 that he or she will die tonight. If he or she is 40 the odds are 180,000 to 1.[6]

The key is inviting people to small group activities or where there are only one or two additional people besides yourself – perhaps a dinner out with two couples, a picnic involving several families, and the list goes on. (At the end of this chapter we are providing a list of suggested activities that can be used to help establish a three-way relationship.) I do not suggest that you avoid church activities with your friends. On the contrary, large church services work because they do not require them to be interactive. But in the beginning, until you have established several more relationships between those individuals and other people in your church, these activities should be the exception rather than the rule. As your friends establish more relationships with people in the church, they will become more receptive to attending functions with larger groups of people simply because the relationships established within that group now make it less of a threat to them.

Also, *The 7 Touches* must not always involve a third party. Remember, there are many things, that have nothing to do with a third party, you can do to strengthen your relationships and show people that you care about them. As you review this list of activities, you will see that many can be done with two or three people as well as with small groups. With a balance of your personal efforts and the touches of other third parties, the church can reach them more quickly.

The 3 Hearings

The principle of saturation also works with the presentation of the Gospel. Many times we think that if we could only get our friends to come to church with us, they would hear the Gospel, instantly be convicted of their sin, converted, and saved. However, research shows that when people make a decision the first time they come to church, only a minimal amount (less than 1%) will stick to that decision. The same research shows that people who hear three presentations of the Gospel are more apt to make a decision that sticks. Therefore, in working with a prospect, make certain the individual sits under at least three different presentations of the Gospel. A *hearing* may be your testimony or the testimony of a friend; attending a *Friend Day*, an Easter or Christmas program, a revival service or a Gospel concert. At the end of this chapter is a list of activities to which you can invite your prospects so they may hear a presentation of the Gospel. However, do not get too pushy. The goal should still be to communicate the Gospel only at the earliest point of receptivity.

Other Uses for the Principles

Bonding people into *receptive/redemptive* relationships is the key to all relationship evangelism. The principle of *The 7 Touches* can be used with a variety of approaches. Following, we have listed three: 1)

The 7 Touches for Laity. This is an unstructured list of ideas and suggestions of things that you can use to strengthen your relationship and rapport with a prospect. 2) *The 7 Touches for Evangelists and Leaders.* This is a more structured use of the law of *The 7 Touches* and can be used more effectively by outgoing individuals in the church such as pastors, professional staff, people with the gift of evangelism, etc. 3) *The 7 Touches of Calvary.*[7] An innovative way showing how one church utilizes this principle.

The 7 Touches for Laity

Inviting the Prospect to:

☐ Dinner   ☐ A Picnic

☐ Bowling   ☐ Tennis

☐ Raquetball   ☐ Athletic Club

☐ Golf   ☐ Church Services

☐ Homecoming   ☐ Friend Day

☐ Gospel Sings   ☐ Class Fellowship/Game Time

☐ Home for Dessert and Visit   ☐ Go Skating with Kids

☐ Fishing   ☐ Swimming

☐ A Park and Sight-seeing   ☐ A Tupperware-type Party

☐ A Birthday Party   ☐ A Ball Game

☐ A Craft Workshop   ☐ Vacation Bible School

☐ A Seasonal Banquet   ☐ A Special Seminar

☐ Revival Service   ☐ Visit a Nursing Home

☐ Go Shopping   ☐ Other_____

Offering to:

☐ Provide transportation if the person's car is in the shop

☐ Provide a meal when the person is sick or has had a death in the family

☐ Baby-sit to give the person a break or allow him a night out for a special occasion

☐ Clean house for a mother who has just had a baby

☐ Feed a pet while the neighbor is on vacation

☐ Mow the yard for the man who has hurt his back or broken a leg

☐ Help meet a financial need, if able

☐ Other_____

Sending cards:

☐ On Birthday   ☐ On Anniversary

☐ At Christmas   ☐ At Easter

☐ At Thanksgiving   ☐ When person is ill

☐ To congratulate for a special event or accomplishment

☐ If person has a death in family   ☐ Other_____

☐ When person is feeling down   ☐ Other_____

The 7 Touches for Evangelists and Leaders

This is a more structured use of the principle of *The 7 Touches*. It assumes that we are dealing with an individual who visited a Sunday morning service. Following is a summary from *Winning the Winnable* by Elmer Towns.[8]

1. *Touch One*: On Sunday afternoon, the pastor should phone those who visited the Sunday morning service; not for the purpose of inviting them to come back, but as a pastor to offer his assistance to them.

2. *Touch Two*: Sunday evening the church secretary should send a personal welcome letter from the pastor to each visitor.

3. *Touch Three*: Monday or Tuesday the secretary should phone and make an appointment for the pastor or member of the visitation task group to visit the home.

4. *Touch Four*: The secretary should mail a letter to confirm the visitation appointment and thank the newcomer for his or her hospitality.

5. *Touch Five*: The pastor or or member from the visitation task force will visit the home.

6. *Touch Six*: After the visit, send a follow-up letter. It should explain how easy it is to receive Christ and/or join the church.

7. *Touch Seven*: On Saturday evening, someone should be appointed to make a phone call to invite the prospect to the Sunday service.

The 7 Touches at Calvary

The principle of the *The 7 Touches* can also be used at the local church facilities. The following is an organized approach used by Rev. Dave Janney at Shiloh Baptist Church in Atlanta, Georgia. It is called *The 7 Touches at the Local Church.*

Beginning with the Visitor (Guest):

1. Parking lot host to escorts guest to sidewalk

2. Sidewalk host greets guest

3. Front door host or hostess greets guest

4. Host or hostess inside church introduces himself or herself

5. Host or hostess escorts guests to welcome center

6. Welcome center hostess: If during Sunday School time, hostess introduces guest to Sunday School representative. If during worship service, hostess introduces guest to usher.

   Also, at this time, hostess supplies guest with information about the church and has guest fill out guest card (check for important information).

7. Class representative escorts guest to Sunday School or usher escorts guest to worship service

It is important to remember to position yourself in strategic places. Be aware of all visitors and make them feel at home. Never let visitors become isolated or unconnected.

The 3 Hearings

Suggested 3 Hearings:

☐ Personal Testimonies   ☐ Evangelistic Services

☐ Tracts   ☐ Gospel Sings

☐ Listening to Christian Music ☐ Seeing a Christian Movie

☐ Attending a Group Bible Study ☐ Youth Rallies

☐ Personal Presentations of the Gospel

☐ Watching a Christian TV Special

☐ Attending a Class Get-together

☐ Friend Day or Other Attendance Campaigns

Editor's note: The principles of *The 7 Touches* and *The 3 Hearings* are based on averages. While in rare cases some people may require only 3 touches or 1 hearing, many others will require 20 touches or 8 hearings. The average is 7 and 3. The point is, do not become impatient if your friend does not respond according to a mechanical plan. Continue on, because they will respond.

In a Nutshell

If we confront someone with the Gospel the first time we meet them, we will most likely offend them and turn them off to us. However, bonding draws people to the church and gets them to stick. It involves building relationships with people outside the church first in order to network them into the church. This is important because the more relationships newcomers have within the church, the greater their potential of staying.

TEAM Evangelism realizes that in order to bond someone to church and reach them for Christ, you must first win them to you; second, to your church; and third (and most important), to Christ. We must begin with *The 7 Touches* to build relationships, then incorporate *The 3 Hearings* to present the Gospel.

TEAM MATE INSTRUCTIONS

Along with each personal prospect listing, beginning on page 24 of *TEAM Mate,* is a page for you to check off *The 7 Touches* and *The 3 Hearings* given to your personal prospect. Each time you give a "touch" or know that your personal prospect has heard the Gospel, mark the appropriate box. There is a place at the bottom of the page to write in when your personal prospect accepts Christ and when he or she begins to attend church regularly. When this is complete you need to add a new personal prospect to your list.

FOOTNOTES

[1] Towns, Elmer, *Winning the Winnable* (Church Growth Institute, Lynchburg, VA: 1987), Page 8.

[2] Bryson, O.J., *Networking the Kingdom,* (Word Publishing, Dallas, TX: 1990), Page 127.

[3] Towns, *Winning,* Page 8.

[4] Arn, Win and W. Charles, *The Master's Plan for Making Disciples* (Church Growth Press, Pasadena, CA: 1982), Pages 155-156.

[5] Arn, *The Master's Plan,* Page 131.

[6] Source: 1990 *Commissioners Ordinary Standard Mortality Tables.*

[7] Towns, Elmer, *How to Reach the Baby Boomer* (Church Growth Institute, Lynchburg, VA: 1990), Vol. 1, Page 36.

[8] Towns, *Winning,* Pages 58 -60.

Chapter Seven

REVIEW QUESTIONS

1. The Gospel must be _____; it can never be
   _____.

2. What is bonding? Why is it important?

3. What is the principle of *The 7 Touches? The 3 Hearings?*

DISCUSSION QUESTIONS

1. How many friends did you make during the first six months of
   your church life? How did this impact your church attendance?

2. Would you be comfortable using the principles of *The 7 Touches*
   and *The 3 Hearings?* How can you exercise your gift in using
   these principles?

3. What are some events or things your church can do to make the
   principle of *The 3 Hearings* most effective?

Chapter 8

THE PRINCIPLE OF READINESS

You're having a discussion with your friend, John, when the subject of religion comes up. John says, "I don't need Christ. I'm doing fine without Him. I'm not even sure He's real. Besides, what could He possibly do for me that I can't do for myself?" What should you do? What would you do?

You could ignore the comment and change the subject because you're afraid to speak up or because you're not sure of what to say. But would that be the right course of action? Should you try to convince your friend of his need for Christ? Should you share a testimony about what Christ has done for you? How would you handle this opportunity? Every Christian should be prepared for situations such as this. But how?

Salespeople and Order-takers

Are you a "salesperson" for Christ?[1] Off the top of our heads, we think that only trained and experienced *salespeople* make sales. When we analyze true selling, we realize that a very small percentage of sales are actually done by salespeople. The majority of sales in the American store are done by an *order-taker*. What is the difference between an order-taker and a salesperson?

A *salesperson* is an individual who can get an order when the person he is selling to is really not ready to buy or is not convinced that now is the time to buy or is not convinced that this is the right product to buy. But the salesperson, through his abilities of persuasion, can get the individual to give him the order at that time.

On the other hand, an *order-taker* is a person who can write the order when the individual knows what he wants, knows when he is ready to buy it, and has made most of the decisions himself. The order-taker can now write the order.

Stop and think for a moment about the last ten items you purchased, not just the last big items, such as an automobile or house (these items are most always sold by salespeople), but think of the items you purchased in the department store – clothing, housewares, etc. – when a so-called salesperson helped you. Was this person a *salesperson* or an *order-taker*? Chances are that he or she was an order-taker because you were ready to buy. You just needed someone to help you find the right size, color, and price range, and so forth. In fact, when a "salesperson" is there pushing you to make the purchase, you usually get irritated.

The same is true with the gift of evangelism. As stated earlier, approximately 10 percent of the people in the church have the gift of evangelism. These people, like the salesperson, are persuasive and may be able to get people to make decisions when they are not prepared to make them. But, the real power in the church lies in the 90 percent who do not have the gift of evangelism, simply because we have nine times as many contacts as the evangelist. We are not considered to be pushy. However, we can influence people to make the right decision and we can answer questions when necessary. *We just need to learn how to be good order-takers.*

So what is the difference between a *good* order-taker and a *bad* order-taker? If you think back to some of your shopping experience, you probably remember the bad order-takers when you asked for a particular item, and they shrugged their shoulders and said, "I don't know. I just work here." They may have gone to find an order for you and brought out the wrong size. Or they did not pay any attention to what you wanted and got everything mixed up. On the other hand, good order-takers know their job and their product. When you ask a question, they give you an immediate answer. They are helpful and say, "Let me find that for you. I don't have the color here, but I am sure I have it in the back room. I know that doesn't fit, but I can have alterations done."

Good order-takers in the church know their product as well. They know the *Gospel*, the presentation of the Gospel, their own testimony, and are able to share it with other people. For this reason, every Christian should have a clear presentation of the Gospel and be able to share the death, burial, and Resurrection of Jesus Christ. Also, they should plan and rehearse so they are familiar enough with their testimony to present it in a way that it will be easily understood by others who need to hear it.

Though most Christians (about 90%) do not have the gift of evangelism, all Christians should be prepared to define their faith anytime an opportunity avails itself – to give reason for their faith or explain why they are a Christian. In fact, the Bible instructs us to be ready. "But sanctify the Lord God in your hearts: and be **ready** always to give an answer to every man that asketh you a reason of the **hope** that is in you...." (1 Peter 3:15). The word "hope" means *faith*. Romans 8:24 states, "For we are saved by hope."

Your Personal Testimony

Every Christian has a personal testimony of how God saved him or her. One testimony may not be as dramatic as another, but all Christians have one. Besides our salvation experience, our testimony may include what God has done for us since we accepted Christ as Saviour or tell of special occasions when God has answered prayer, met a need, or brought us through difficult times. We may tell how God has changed our lives. Your own testimony may not be your original salvation experience, but your renewed commitment to Christ. It doesn't have to be your salvation experience at all. You might want to tell about what happened when you really got serious and decided to do things His way or started letting the Word of God become your guide for daily living.

A lot of times you may not think you are really giving a testimony because what you are saying is not spiritual enough. You may believe that you must be filled with emotion and use just the right words, coming from the pages of Scripture to be giving a testimony. But this is not so. In fact, sometimes we make our testimonies so spiritual and scriptural that our Christian language does not relate to a lost person. Remember, they have not been going to church for years like most of us and have a totally different vocabulary. Being *too* spiritual can scare them off. In any respect you must be prepared to share whatever you feel will demonstrate the love and grace of God that will show your friend why you have faith in God.

Your Own Gospel Presentation

In addition to your testimony, you need your own personal presentation of the Gospel. No *single* presentation is the only one. Use any presentation as long as it clearly reveals the death, burial, and Resurrection of Jesus Christ. You may be comfortable with the *Romans Road*, the *Four Spiritual Laws* or some other common Gospel presentation. You may even have your own compilation of Scriptures and comments to show someone how to receive Christ as Saviour. If I were going to lead someone to Christ, I could not use the *Four Spiritual Laws*. I can't remember what they are. Nor, could I use the *Romans Road*. I'm not sure of all the points. However, I could take anyone to Acts 16:31 and expand upon, "Believe on the Lord Jesus Christ, and thou shalt be saved." By explaining the original definition of the word "believe," which means, "to totally rely upon." I could share with someone what it means to totally rely upon Christ as Saviour. Remember, it is not necessary for us to dot every "i" and cross every "t," nor understand every point in the outline of the Doctrine of Salvation. If this were necessary, there would be many of us who could not lay our own claim to salvation.

If you do not already have a specific presentation that you use, you need to prepare one and become familiar with it. Be sure to jot it down and keep it updated in your *TEAM Mate* book. Remember to be *prepared!*

Training for Personal Evangelism

Possibly the most creative area of Christianity is the ability of Christians to give excuses for not showing up for a personal evangelism training class. If you dig deep enough and are willing to lead the questions you can get the truth as to why people do not want to come. The average Christian views personal evangelism training classes as second cousin to the medieval torture chamber. Their perception as to what goes on in these training programs keeps them away, all in a mode of self-defense. Most believe they will be put on the spot or embarrassed. They fear that someone will call on them to pray or that they are going to be forced to visit strangers. Most believe only the bold and fearless should attend. Unfortunately, in most cases they are right. One instructor rebuked me by saying, "No one in my group has those type problems." But the problem is not with the handfuls that show up. It is with the mobs that stay away.

I believe *every* Christian would benefit from a personal evangelism training class. However, I do not believe every Christian should participate in the same type of program.

For People *with* the Gift of Evangelism

1. The first type of program that should be offered is for people with the gift of evangelism. Two of the most popular programs today are *Evangelism Explosion (EE)* and *Continuous Witness Training (CWT)*. Church Growth Institute has a program available called *Night of Caring (NOC)*. Many other visitation-type programs exist. These programs, when coupled with an understanding of the *TEAM Philosophy of Ministry,* are excellent tools for training people with the gift of evangelism. Remember *TEAM Evangelism* has not eliminated the visitation program. It suggests that you only put people with suitable gifts in it. Therefore, if you do not have the gift of evangelism, I suggest that you participate in a different type of program that is not geared toward an outgoing or confrontational personality.

Because so many suitable programs are available for training people with the gift of evangelism, I will go no further than to point out that when you select one of these programs, notice that few really recognize the gift of evangelism. Most of these programs assume that all Christians can participate. You must allow for this omission when using those programs.

For People *without* the Gift of Evangelism

2. *How do you share Christ with a friend when you don't have the gift of evangelism?* I don't want to leave you with the impression that you never need to verbalize your faith. As pointed out earlier, one of the major weaknesses of Lifestyle Evangelism is that people think that if they live clean lives, their lifestyles will be their witness and they never have to verbalize anything. Plus, my arguments against *everyone* being involved in Confrontational Evangelism may also lead you to think you don't need to verbalize. On the contrary. *You don't need to be confrontational, but you still need to verbalize your faith when the opportunities arise.* This is being a witness. Acts 1:8 says, "Ye shall be *witnesses* unto me...." If we are to be witnesses then what is a witness? You may already have a perception of the word in your mind. I have seen definitions that range from "living a good life" to "you need to be winning three souls a week to Christ." Acts 22:15 states, "For thou shalt be his witness unto all men of what thou hast *seen* and *heard*." The words seen and heard seem to be keys in this passage. *A witness is one who gives testimony of what he or she has seen or heard.*

Just like in a courtroom, a witness gives testimony of what he or she has seen and heard. And also like in a courtroom, a witness gives testimony when he or she is put on the stand or questioned. A witness never needs to go from door to door testifying to everyone. *But* every witness needs to be prepared to give his testimony when called upon. Even still, I think we should go one step further. If you were sitting in a courtroom and knew your testimony would make a difference in the outcome of a trial, you would feel the obligation to speak up, even if you were not called on. Sometimes as Christians we must do the same.

At this point, you might say to me, "Look, I buy this whole concept of TEAM Evangelism, but I am not going to let you trick me into making verbal presentations of the Gospel to my friends. I would not want to say it publicly, but when I am honest with myself, I'm just not going to do that." If that is the way you feel, that's fine, but don't let me drive you away from doing what you can. I pray that if you are not going to make any direct attempts to lead your personal prospects to Christ, you will key in on *The 3 Hearings* and do all you can do to see that they will hear several presentations of the Gospel. Remember, it is not necessary for *you* to present the Gospel to them for them to get saved, but it is necessary for *someone* to present the Gospel to them.

I do realize though that many people without the gift of evangelism would like to know how to share their faith or present the Gospel. They would not mind going through a personal evangelism class if it would help them do a better job of verbalizing their faith. Yet, at the same time, they want absolutely nothing to do with any form of visitation program. This group needs an entirely different type of approach or approaches to sharing than those with the gift of evangelism. Therefore, programs like *EE, CWT,* or *NOC* will not only fail to get results with this group, but their perceptions of the programs will keep them from coming in the first place.

That is why I recommend training programs that are designed for "order-takers" not "salespeople." One such program is *Living Proof*, published by NavPress. Church Growth Institute is making this program available along with several others ranging in method from outreach Bible studies to lifestyle witnessing (see Appendix 3).

Leaders need to make these types of programs available to the laity on a nonthreatening level. Otherwise, the laity will not attend. The teacher should always make it clear that no one will be unexpectedly called to pray or forced to memorize verses and quote them back to the rest of the group or be sent out to present the Gospel or do anything that will embarrass them or put them on the spot without first getting their permission. Furthermore, there needs to be a promise that no tricks or pressure will be used to get each individual's permission. In essence all the student needs to do is just sit, listen, and take notes. This practical teaching will help you overcome much of your fear of witnessing. It will make it easier for you to witness to those people within your sphere of influence – those whom you really feel it is necessary to reach or whom God has convicted you to witness to. In any respect, when and if the day comes that you present the Gospel to someone, you will find that this training made it much easier for you.

Let me end with a statement I have made several times before in this text. With *TEAM Evangelism,* you may not be the one who prays the sinner's prayer with a lost person, but you can play a vital role in helping that person take one more step closer to accepting Christ; and the best part of all is, you only have to be *yourself.*

In a Nutshell

Although every Christian is not required to confront someone with the Gospel, every Christian does have a responsibility to "be *ready* always to give an answer to every man that asketh you a reason of the hope that is in you" (1 Peter 3:15).

TEAM *Evangelism* teaches team members to be prepared – to write down and become familiar with their own testimonies and personal presentations of the Gospel. Team members should be ready at all times to give a testimony and Gospel presentation in case the opportunity to do so arises.

Although a personal evangelism training class is not a part of this program, TEAM *Evangelism* believes it would behoove every Christian to participate in one of several programs. Those with the gift of evangelism should participate in a visitation-type program while those without the gift of evangelism should participate in a milder and less confrontational-type program that will make it easier for them to share their faith when opportunities arise.

TEAM MATE INSTRUCTIONS

Page 40 of TEAM *Mate* gives you the opportunity and space to write out your own personal testimony. Page 42 is for composing your own presentation of the Gospel. Once you have written and rewritten these presentations to your satisfaction, become familiar with them. Your will then be ready and able to be a "good order-taker."

FOOTNOTES

[1] I am aware that secular and business terms ruffle the feathers of many Christians when used in conjunction with the church. I fully understand that we do not sell Jesus Christ like we would a hamburger or a car. However, I do not apologize for the use of the terms, because I am convinced that people readily relate to them, which makes it easier to get my point across. Scripturalizing the terms would not change their meaning, but would only make it harder to communicate the principle.

Chapter Eight

REVIEW QUESTIONS

1. What is the difference between an order-taker and a salesperson?

2. How does this compare with those in the church who have the gifts of evangelism and those who do not?

3. Why should the church provide more than one type of personal evangelism training program?

DISCUSSION QUESTIONS

1. Are you an order-taker or a salesperson? Why?

2. How can you improve your order-taking or sales methods?

3. Your church's order-taking and sales abilities are important. Do you have any suggestions of how the team can work together more effectively to ensure good salesmanship? Do you believe a personal evangelism course would improve your team? How?

Appendix 1

SPIRITUAL GIFTS INVENTORY

The Spiritual Gifts Inventory is not a test, but an inventory showing your strengths and weaknesses in the nine task-oriented gifts God has given Christians. Its purpose is to help you recognize your dominant spiritual gift and offer you guidance as to where you might best serve in the local church – which is the only true way to determine your spiritual gifts.

Your answers should reflect your feelings and desires, not what you consider your duty. Christian duties often require a person to perform where he or she is not gifted.

Read each following statement and decide how it pertains to you. Then on the Spiritual Gifts Inventory Answer Sheet, darken in the circle that most accurately applies to you. If the statement fits you 70% to 100% of the time, darken in circle (1) Almost Always. If the statement fits you 40% to 70% of the time, darken in circle (2) Occasionally. If the statement fits you less than 40% of the time, darken in circle (3) Not Very Often.

To determine where your strengths lie, separate the answer sheets and follow the instructions on page 2. When you have completed the Inventory, review the evaluation in Appendix 2.

If you do not have an answer sheet, see the order form in the back of this text.

Questionnaire (Do not mark on this. Use your answer sheet.)

1. I have a consuming passion for lost souls.

2. I put great importance on repentance.

3. I believe I am very discerning of other people's motives.

4. When I speak, I wish to sir the consciences of others.

5. I have an unusually strong desire to study the Word of God.

6. I put great importance on education.

7. When I do something, I like to see "tangible" results for my efforts.

8. When I speak to a group, my message usually deals with topics, not verse-by-verse studies.

9. I am willing to assume a long-term personal responsibility for the spiritual welfare of a group of believers.

10. I am people centered. I need many relationships in my life.

11. I am usually soft spoken.

12. I am patient, but am willing to respond to other's needs quickly.

13. I am fulfilled by performing routine tasks in the church for God's glory.

14. I am usually involved in a variety of activities that help other people.

15. I keep myself and my business affairs well organized.

16. I have a burden to support missions.

17. I make decisions based strictly on facts and proven data.

18. I can communicate goals in a way that others may fulfill them.

19. I believe salvation is the greatest gift of all.

20. Some people think my witnessing tactics are pushy.

21. I can spot sin when other people can't.

22. I feel a great need to expose sin in others.

23. I like to use visuals and books to support me when I am speaking.

24. I am constantly analyzing for ways to do and say things better.

25. I believe I am a very practical person.

26. I am able to help others when they have personal problems.

27. I am willing to spend large amounts of time in prayer for other people.

28. I enjoy looking after the spiritual welfare of others. I am protective.

29. I find it very easy to express my feelings.

30. I have a real burden to comfort others.

31. I prefer to be out of the public eye to be fulfilled.

32. I am burdened with the physical needs of others.

33. When I give, I want it to be a private matter between me and God.

34. I am sensitive to the financial and material needs of others.

35. I am goal oriented, as opposed to being people or content oriented.

36. I work best under pressure.

37. I have a desire to meet lost people, even when they are total strangers.

38. I would rather witness than do anything else.

39. I am impatient with the wrong actions of others.

40. I am disorganized and must depend on others to keep me on schedule.

41. I have an organized system to store facts and figures.

42. I am more concerned with the content of material rather than with people or the task.

43. When studying Scripture, I am more interested in the practical areas.

44. I put great importance on the will of God.

45. I have a burden to see others learn and grow.

46. I am more relationship oriented than task oriented.

47. I am sympathetic and sensitive with others.

48. Other people think I am weak because of my lack of firmness.

49. I enjoy working with my hands.

50. I often let people talk me into things I don't want to do.

51. I am always ready and willing to give if a valid need exists.

52. I have the ability to make quick decisions concerning finances.

53. I do things promptly. I make decisions quickly.

54. I dream big dreams, although I don't always share them with others.

55. I have a clear understanding of the Gospel message and can easily relate it to others.

56. I am socially active and get along well with others at all times.

57. I must verbalize (speak) my message. I would never be content only writing it.

58. I always speak with urgency and want others to make quick decisions.

59. Sometimes I would rather just write, but "must teach" because others would not present my material correctly.

60. The use of a verse out of context upsets me.

61. I have several steps of action to solve every problem.

62. I question the value of deep doctrinal studies.

63. I am very protective of people under my care.

64. Teaching the same material over and over is a drag for me.

65. I try to always appear loving.
66. I act on emotions rather than logic.
67. I am impressed when exhorted to serve.
68. I like to meet needs immediately.
69. When giving, I always like my gift to be of high quality.
70. Other people think I am materialistic because of the importance I put on money.
71. I delegate whenever and wherever possible, but I know when and where I can't.
72. I am willing to attempt impossible tasks for God.
73. I take great joy in seeing men and women come to Christ.
74. I believe soulwinning is the greatest responsibility given to every Christian.
75. I enjoy speaking in public, and do it with boldness.
76. I am burdened to memorize Scripture.
77. I have a tendency to question the knowledge of those who teach me.
78. Others accuse me of giving too many details.
79. I have the ability to motivate others.
80. Unpractical teaching upsets me.
81. I wish to give direction to those under my care.
82. I am willing to study whatever is necessary in order to feed those I am working with.
83. My heart goes out to the poor, the aged, the ill, the under-privileged, etc.
84. I seem to attract people who are hurting or rejoicing.
85. I am already helping people while others are still talking about it.
86. I am quick to respond to others' need for help.
87. I want to know my financial gift is being used properly.
88. I may judge others' success by the amount of their material assets.
89. I want to be a winner. I cannot bear defeat.
90. I am capable of making quick decisions and sticking to them.
91. When I witness to a lost person I always press for a decision.
92. Others think I am more interested in numbers than in people.

93. You must "prove" me wrong before I will go along with you.

94. Studying is not my bag. I rely on others to do background work for me.

95. I find other teachers' material hard to present. I prefer to develop my own lessons.

96. I put great emphasis on word pronunciation.

97. Other people think I am not evangelistic because of my emphasis on personal growth.

98. I am accused of not using enough Scripture when teaching.

99. I enjoy doing a wide variety of activities without being confined to one.

100. I perceive myself as a shepherd.

101. I am an emotional person. I cry easily.

102. I identify emotionally and mentally with others.

103. Some people think I neglect spiritual needs.

104. I enjoy mechanical jobs in the church.

105. I may measure others' spirituality by the amount of their giving.

106. Others think I am trying to control them with my money.

107. When there is no leadership in a group, I will assume it.

108. I have the ability to organize and harmonize the people I work with.

END

Appendix 2

EVALUATING YOUR SPIRITUAL GIFTS INVENTORY

Now that you have taken the Inventory, you can see where your strengths are.

Overall low scores usually indicate a low self-esteem. Understanding the principles and the development of your spiritual gifts and their relationships to personal ministry should help increase self-esteem. Also, overall low scores can confirm the gift of showing mercy since one of the characteristics of that gift is a tendency toward low self-esteem.

Overall high scores usually indicate high self-esteem. It can also confirm the gifts of teaching, prophecy or administration since they are sometimes characterized by a tendency toward high self-esteem.

Extremely high and low scores with large separations between highs and lows usually indicate decisiveness and in some cases, a confirmation of the gift of administration. It may also be an indication that you pretty much know what God wants you to do and where you are headed with your life.

An overall high score or even score in all gifts usually indicates the gift of pastor/shepherd if pastor/shepherd is one of your high scores.

It is not unusual for women to score very high in the area of pastor/shepherd because the characteristics of pastor/shepherd are also characteristics of mothering, which is a natural tendency for women.

Some people with the gift of pastor/shepherd will also score high in showing mercy because of the strong shepherding desire. Others will score high in teaching or exhortation because of the teaching desire.

People with high scores in directly opposite gifts (prophet/mercy, server/administrator) usually become unique individuals with an unusually high achievement and/or attraction about their ministries.

Interaction between your dominant and secondary gifts is important. Chapter 3 of this text examines spiritual gifts, the tools of ministry. If you desire further information on spiritual gifts, consult your pastor or obtain a copy of the *TEAM Ministry* text by Larry Gilbert. *TEAM Ministry* is a spiritual gifts study. It tells what spiritual gifts are, shows common characteristics of each gift, and shows how they work together in local church ministry.

We recommend that you give the second answer sheet enclosed with this book to a friend who knows you well. Ask the friend to go through the Spiritual Gifts Inventory and mark the answer sheet the way he or she believes you should answer it, based on his or her perspective of you. Compare answers. This may help you realize things you did not see in yourself and will help you better evaluate your own gifts and abilities.

Appendix 3

TEAM EVANGELISM RESOURCES

Church Growth Institute has designed several resources that will guide you through *TEAM Evangelism* and help you effectively implement it into your church. The following simple outline of resources will show you what is available and how they work.

1. *TEAM Evangelism: Giving New Meaning to Lay Evangelism.* This textbook starts with a *church growth* philosophy, teaches the principles of evangelism that are known to work, shows how every member of the church can participate in an ongoing evangelistic effort, and frees them to participate by relieving guilt. Every family should have a copy. Each textbook is sold with a copy of *TEAM Mate* and two Spiritual Gifts Inventory answer sheets.

2. *TEAM Mate: Personal Ministry Planner.* This booklet is the very heart of *TEAM Evangelism.* It is the actual *application* of the principles taught. This tracking tool simply organizes people to follow through on the principles in a low-keyed but continual manner. It keeps them in touch with the needs of people around them who need to know Christ. Several sections in *TEAM Mate* are designed for interactive participation. This ties the application to the church and gives the pastor some control and accountability. Every church member should have his or her own copy of *TEAM Mate* and should receive a new one yearly.

3. *TEAM Evangelism Resource Packet.* The resource packet contains two manuals. The *Teacher's Manual* explains how to teach a workshop or eight-week extended class on *TEAM Evangelism.* This part of the packet contains masters for overhead transparencies, a workbook that can be copied as lesson handouts, a sample Spiritual Gifts Inventory, and audiocassettes of actual *TEAM Evangelism* lectures. The *Implementation Manual* provides a systematic strategy for incorporating *TEAM Evangelism* into your church. It shows leaders how to structure *TEAM Evangelism* in order to utilize its principles and application. It shows the pastor how he can *make it happen.* Ultimately the burden for success or failure rests on his shoulders. This manual spells out additional leadership principles the pastor should know, gives a master calendar and reproducible forms, provides ideas on promotion to get the greatest participation

and attendance, plus shows how to maintain overall accountability while serving as the leader.

4. *TEAM Evangelism in Action.* This inexpensive newsletter is published monthly and sold to the church in bulk. It should be passed out to all members, used as a bulletin insert or made available in the lobby. It keeps a fresh supply of new ideas coming to your people on how to strengthen relationships and deal with specific problems and gives many simple suggestions on how laypeople can use the principles of *TEAM Evangelism.* It also contains testimonies and stories of people who have used *TEAM Evangelism* successfully.

5. *Local Church Seminars.* Church Growth Institute is developing a network of local church instructors. If you are interested in having an experienced instructor come to your church to help you initiate *TEAM Evangelism,* contact the Seminar Department at Church Growth Institute, P.O. Box 4404, Lynchburg, VA 24502.

6. *TEAM Ministry: A Guide to Spiritual Gifts and Lay Involvement.* *TEAM Evangelism* revolves around the philosophy of ministry taught in *TEAM Ministry* (using people where they are most usable). The chart, *The TEAM vs. The Lost,* which is the very heart of the *TEAM Ministry* program, has been copied from *TEAM Ministry.* Although we have made every effort to allow each resource to stand on its own and not to make *TEAM Ministry* a prerequisite for *TEAM Evangelism,* we still recommend that you teach *TEAM Ministry* to your people. Their understanding of the principles taught in *TEAM Ministry* will add to their self-acceptance and understanding of the church and its function and of how God has uniquely equipped each one to work in the ministry. Applying *TEAM Ministry* principles will add to the overall success in their lives and church. People who are familiar with these principles will "catch on" to *TEAM Evangelism* much faster.

7. *Night of Caring: Equipping for Visitation Evangelism.* This training program, by Paul Cedar, shows people how to do effective visitation. It is an outstanding tool for training people with the gift of evangelism. The packet contains a participant workbook, facilitator's manual, and 12 sessions on VHS videotape.

8. *Living Proof: A Small Group Video Series.* Written by Jim Petersen, this resource contains a 12-lesson videotape series teaching how people without the gift of evangelism can stair-step people to Christ. Includes participant workbook, two videotapes, and a leader's lesson plan.

9. *Outreach Bible Study: Team Training for Evangelistic Bible Studies.* Another tool by Paul Cedar for those without the gift of evangelism, this book can move your ministry of evangelism off your church campus into the "turf" of the outsider – a home, office, college campus, factory, or even a coffee shop. It contains a facilitator's manual and a student manual with six videotaped sessions.

From time to time, Church Growth Institute will produce other programs that support the *TEAM Philosophy of Ministry* .

GLOSSARY

ADMINISTRATION, THE GIFT OF: People with the gift of administration have the Spirit-given capacity and desire to serve God by organizing, administering, promoting, and leading the various affairs of the church.

BAPTISM: Baptizing is part of the Great Commission as stated in Matthew 28:19, "...baptizing them in the name of the Father, and of the Son, and of the Holy Ghost." Although different denominations disagree doctrinally on whether baptism is submersion or sprinkling, functionally we all agree it equals identification with the body of Christ or the local church. Therefore, baptizing also means getting people churched.

BIBLICAL PROCEDURE FOR TRAINING CHRISTIANS: The Biblical Procedure for Training Christians is found in 2 Timothy 3:16-17. "All scripture is given by inspiration of God, and is profitable for doctrine, for reproof, for correction, for instruction in righteousness: that the man of God may be perfect, thoroughly furnished unto all good works." We are to use Scripture to teach doctrine (what to believe), to reprove (confront sin), to correct (show the alternative action to sin), and to instruct in righteousness (how to live) with importance placed on the order in which they appear in verse 16.

BONDING, THE PRINCIPLE OF: Bonding is getting people to stick to the church. How? Through building relationships. The principle of bonding says that the more relationships newcomers have within the church the greater their potential of staying; the fewer relationships they have within the church, the more apt they are to leave.

BURDEN: What is a burden? A motivating force from within that makes a demand on your resources, whether material (1 Thess. 2:6) or emotional; an insatiable hunger gnawing at your soul; a burning in your heart to do what God has called you to do.

CONFRONTATIONAL EVANGELISM: This type of evangelism compels the Christian to confront every lost person he or she meets with the Gospel. Witnessing goes beyond personal testimony, and requires presenting the Gospel and pressing for a decision every time. Confrontational Evangelism believes that it is necessary to get a commitment for Christ in order to be successful, so the method revolves around a presentation of the Gospel. Confrontational Evangelism is designed for those with the gift of evangelism.

DIMINISHING PROSPECTS, THE PRINCIPLE OF: Prospects are people with whom we have existing relationships. They are people we love and care about. They are usually receptive to us. Every person has a limited number of prospects, usually at least seven. The principle of the diminishing prospect states that the longer people are Christians the less prospects they have because within their sphere of influence, there are less people who are not churched or saved.

EPHESIANS 4 PASTOR: The steward of the gifts, talents, and abilities of those entrusted to his care.

EVANGELISM, THE GIFT OF: The evangelist, the person with the gift of evangelism, has the Spirit-given capacity and desire to serve God by leading people who are beyond his or her natural sphere of influence to the saving knowledge of Jesus Christ. This person is the aggressive soulwinner who seeks the lost and is comfortable with Confrontational Evangelism.

EVENT EVANGELISM: Surveys show that the number one reason people come to church is for fellowship. People need and enjoy fellowship with others. They are comfortable around those who are friendly. Therefore, it is necessary for us to be friendly and build good relationships. Event Evangelism involves building relationships and inviting those with whom we have relationships to special events.

EXHORTATION: Exhorters are people who have the gift of exhortation. They have the Spirit-given capacity and desire to serve God by motivating others to action by urging them to pursue a course of conduct. These people are "how-to" teachers, giving the practical application of God's Word. They help put principles into practice. Exhorters also make good counselors because they are willing to spend time with people and offer them practical steps to solving their problems.

EXTENDED CHURCH, THE PRINCIPLE OF: The principle of the extended church is sometimes called the principle of existing relationships. Every Christian has existing relationships with an average of seven people–seven people whom they care about. Research shows that 86 percent of the people who come to church do so as a result of being invited by a friend or relative. This means that most of the people with whom you have relationships are willing to come to church if you invite them.

EASY-BELIEVISM: Easy-believism is when the salvation experience is explained by an emphasis on the verbal decision, often at the expense of the sinner's actual repentance of his sinful condition. Sometimes when people are pressured into salvation decisions, they only say "yes" to get the soulwinner to leave them alone. They make a hurried decision, not understanding or really feeling the necessity of the decision. This is decision-getting without true conversion. It often leaves people thinking they have accepted Christ, when they have not. People sincerely accept Christ when they realize their need and want to do so.

GIFT AWARENESS: In order to use your spiritual gift and work in the area of ministry in which you best fit, you must be aware of your own spiritual gift and ways it can be exercised. You should also be aware of other members' gifts and how their gifts are exercised in order to effectively minister with them.

GIFT COLONIZATION: Gift colonization is the direct and inescapable result of unrestrained gift gravitation. Christians are often drawn to those who have the same gift they have and sometimes build "colonies" of a certain gift, usually a church full of them, which often extends to "movements" as well.

GIFT DODGING: Gift dodging is the act of trying to dodge the responsibility that comes with your spiritual gift; ignoring the fact that you have a gift and taking for granted its place in God's work.

GIFT GRAVITATION: Gift gravitation is the tendency among Christians to attract and be attracted to other Christians with like spiritual gifts. We like doing things with people who enjoy the same things we enjoy. When someone else has the same spiritual gift as us, we can identify with them. We have something in common. Although it is good to fellowship with those of like gifts, it is necessary to understand and accept the gifts of others.

GIFT IGNORANCE: Gift Ignorance is a lack of knowledge regarding the possession of spiritual gifts and their functions. Every Christian has at least one spiritual gift, given by God, for use in serving Him and ministering to others. Some people have several gifts with one being dominant.

GIFT IMPOSING: Gift Imposing is the act of forcing your spiritual gift upon other Christians and attempting to compel them to perform as though it were God's gift to them as well. Although every Christian has a spiritual gift and some have the same gift, not everyone has the same gift. We cannot expect others to minister exactly like we do and to be effective using the same methods we do. God did not make everyone alike, did not give everyone the same gift or the same personality, and does not expect everyone to be just alike.

GIFT MIX: Gift mix is a belief that the majority of Christians have various gifts, different degrees of giftedness, and many ministries through which to exercise each gift. Mixtures of these elements give each believer personal identity in the body of Christ.

GIVING, THE GIFT OF: Christians with the gift of giving have the Spirit-given capacity and desire to serve God by giving their material resources, far beyond the tithe, to further the work of God. These people meet financial needs of fellow Christians and church members. Givers give to further the work of God, not to show off.

GREAT COMMISSION, THE: The fulfillment of the Great Commission is a procedure that starts by our appealing to individuals who in many cases have only a superficial awareness of God, then stepping them through a growth process with the objective of them becoming Christlike. It is a process in which we reach, baptize, and teach. We do lead people to Christ as we have always believed the Great Commission commanded us to do, but we go beyond that step.

GUILT-TRIP MOTIVATION: Guilt-trip motivation is compelling people to action by placing guilt on them rather than letting the Holy Spirit convict. It is an attitude of making others feel inferior and that they are not right with God.

LIFESTYLE EVANGELISM: Lifestyle Evangelism is a form of non-Confrontational Evangelism; living your life that others might see Christ in you. Many who use this method would say, "Our job is to sow seeds, but not verbal seeds, for actions speak louder than words." They believe everyone should witness through his or her lifestyle.

LITTLE TOE, THE PRINCIPLE OF THE: The little toe has a lot to do with the balance of your body. Even though your little toe has no muscles to stop you from falling if you lean off balance, it immediately sends a signal to the brain that says, "out of balance." Then the brain signals a muscle in the side of the foot to contract and keep you from falling. So without your little toe, you would easily lose your balance and fall. And if the little toe goes to sleep, it affects the whole body. Just like the little toe is necessary to the human body for balance; every believer's spiritual gift is necessary to the church in order to give balance.

MERCY SHOWING, THE GIFT OF: Mercy-showers are people who have the spirit-given capacity and desire to serve God by identifying and comforting those who are in distress. They understand and comfort their fellow Christians. Mercy-showers empathize with others—feel what others are feeling. They are easy to talk to, get along well with others, and are self-sacrificing.

MINISTERING GIFTS: Those who have ministering gifts (pastor/shepherd, mercy-shower, server, giver, administrator) work behind the scenes in support roles to those who have speaking gifts (pastor/shepherd, prophecy, teaching, exhortation, evangelism). Pastor/shepherd falls into both categories because of the duty to pastor and shepherd. People who have ministering gifts enjoy supporting those who have speaking gifts. These ministers are "kingmakers."

PASTOR/SHEPHERD, THE GIFT OF: Pastor/shepherds have the Spirit-given capacity and desire to serve God by overseeing, training, and caring for the needs of a group of Christians. They lead and feed their flocks as well as coach their teams (their churches, classes, etc.).

PAY AND PRAY, THE PRINCIPLE OF: The principle of pay and pray is the idea that "you might not be able to do anything else, but you can always give" or "...but you can always pray." This attitude belittles the gifts of giving and of prayer. It says they are not important. In fact, they are extremely important. Without financial support many programs cannot exist or at least cannot grow and reach their full potential. Without prayer, the program may not even get off to a start. If it does, it will never be nearly as effective as it would if it were bathed in prayer.

PERSONAL MINISTRY: A personal ministry is an activity that you as an individual Christian do for God, to benefit someone else. Each of us can have a personal ministry through using our God-given spiritual gifts.

POTTS PRINCIPLE, THE: The Potts Principle tells us that we cannot rely solely on our lifestyles to witness or influence people for Christ. Many Christians are like Clever Potts, a former professional baseball player who was the catcher for Babe Ruth. A lonely old man, he would tell his "war" stories to get your attention, then work in his own humor. He often said, "Eighty-seven years old (as if he were getting ready to give you his philosophy of life), don't drink, smoke, cuss, chew, fool around with women." Then after a long pause and in a low, drawn-out voice he would say, "S-o-m-e-t-i-m-e-s." Since Christians do what they shouldn't do sometimes, even though they do what is right most of the time, we cannot use only our lifestyles as a witness.

PRAYER, THE PRINCIPLE OF: Prayer is a major, integral part of any evangelism program. It is a crucial part of any ministry. Some people will pray sincerely only for those people they care about most. Others have a special ministry of prayer and the desire to pray for many and much. We can pray individually, privately, publicly, or in prayer groups. As we saturate our evangelistic efforts with prayer by name and need we go directly to God with the needs of the people we care about the most. In turn, God uses prayer as an avenue to show us how to minister to the needs that will ultimately lead those people to salvation and maturity in Christ.

PRESUPPOSITIONS: A presupposition is something assumed, taken for granted. It is a deduction lacking direct evidence. Presuppositions often create barriers to Christians doing effective outreach.

PROPHECY, THE GIFT OF: Prophets, people with the gift of prophecy, have the Spirit-given capacity and desire to serve God by proclaiming God's truth. They are hell-fire and brimstone preachers pointing out sin. When people realize their sin, this preaching results in edification, exhortation, and comfort.

PROSPECTS/SUSPECTS: Prospects are people with whom we have existing relationships. They are those we care about most and sincerely want to lead to Christ. These people are usually our family members (parents, brothers, sisters, children, grandparents, aunts, uncles, cousins, in-laws, and so on), our friends, our neighbors, our co-workers; sometimes our beautician, mailman, doctor, our child's teacher, and the list goes on. It stands to reason that the people we are concerned about and know well are more receptive to us than strangers. Suspects are strangers, people we do not know or people we hardly know. Suspects are not likely to be very receptive to us.

READINESS, THE PRINCIPLE OF: All of us, even those who do not have the gift of evangelism, should be ready to define our faith if anyone asks us to give a reason for our faith or to explain why we are Christians. First Peter 3:15 says, "But sanctify the Lord God in your hearts: and be ready always to give an answer to every man that asketh you a reason of the hope that is in you with meekness and fear." Therefore, the principle of readiness is based on a biblical mandate.

RULE OF SEVEN: The rule of seven is that when a church member has seven close friends in a church, he or she will never leave it (O.J. Bryson, *Networking the Kingdom*). This rule supports the principle of bonding that says the more relationships a newcomer has within the church the greater his or her potential of staying.

SALESPERSONS/ORDER-TAKERS: Salespeople are individuals who can get orders when the people they are selling to are not really ready to buy or are not convinced that now is the time to buy or that this is the right product to buy. Salespeople, through their abilities of persuasion, can get people to give them orders at that time. Evangelists are like salespeople. They are able to present the Gospel and convince people of their need of salvation. They have the ability to persuade people, even strangers, to repent and accept Christ as Saviour. Order-takers write down orders when people know what they want, know when they are ready to buy it, and have made most of the decisions themselves. Order-takers can take and fill the order. Good order-takers are prepared. They know their job and their products. They can give immediate answers about their products. Most of us are order-takers and need to know the Gospel and be ready to give answers about it. We need to be familiar with our own testimonies and be able to share them with others.

SATURATION, THE PRINCIPLE OF: The principle of saturation recognizes that touching someone's life in any area only once will make little impact of influence on them. When we repeatedly have contact with a person, when we "saturate" them with our presence and involve them in our lives, we will have more influence on them.

SERVING, THE GIFT OF: People with the gift of serving have the Spirit-given capacity and desire to serve God by rendering practical help in both physical and spiritual matters. They meet the practical needs of fellow Christians and the church. This gift is actually a combination of helps and ministering. People with this gift enjoy manual work and don't mind working behind the scenes.

SEVEN TOUCHES, THE: According to research, people usually make meaningful decisions for Christ after the church has contacted them seven times. In order to influence people for Christ, we must reach out and touch them seven times (this is an average). *The 7 Touches* draw people into relationships and help bond them to the church.

SOWING & REAPING, THE PRINCIPLE OF: The principle of sowing and reaping is simple: you sow the seed and reap the harvest. We build relationships, influence people, and present our testimonies in order to lead people to Christ. The laity is responsible for planting the seed, watering the seed, cultivating, hoeing, and weeding, but the leader is responsible for the harvest.

SPHERE OF INFLUENCE: Our sphere of influence is those people who are our prospects–people with whom we have existing relationships, receptive individuals. Average Christians work very comfortably within their own sphere of influence. Eighty-six percent of the people who participated in a national survey said they joined a church or were lead to Christ as a result of a friend's or relative's influence. Therefore, our sphere of influence–existing relationships–is the key to growing churches.

SPIRITUAL GIFTS: Spiritual gifts are supernatural capacities and desires to serve God in certain ways. They are graciously given by God at the time of the new birth (salvation/when we accept Christ as Saviour). God accomplishes His work through believers using their spiritual gifts to minister to their fellowman.

STAIR-STEPPING, THE PRINCIPLE OF: Stair-stepping is leading

prospects through a process where they go from having a superficial awareness of God to becoming mature Christians. Somewhere along the way they accept Christ as Saviour and begin to regularly attend church, not necessarily in that order.

TEACHING, THE GIFT OF: People with the gift of teaching have the Spirit-given capacity and desire to serve God by making clear the truth of the Word of God with accuracy and simplicity. They are scholars who clarify the doctrines and teachings of the Bible. They are enthusiastic about explaining things, are easily understood when teaching, and stimulate others to learn.

TEAM: The team is a group of active people empowered by the Holy Spirit and gifted in the various spiritual gifts for the purpose of meeting the needs of people. Every local church should be a team.

TEAM EVANGELISM: TEAM Evangelism is using all the spiritual gifts in a team effort to bring people to Christ, to get them churched, and to lead them to Christian maturity. TEAM Evangelism is a low-key, inoffensive program that shows laity how to plant and cultivate relationships, therefore making them more aware of the people around them who are in need of Christ. The application of the program lies in TEAM Mate, the personal ministry planner. When followed according to the plan, TEAM Evangelism is very effective in reaching people for Christ. It provides a place for those with the gift of evangelism as well as those without the gift of evangelism.

TEAM GIFTS: TEAM gifts, also called "task-oriented" gifts, are functions rather than character qualities. They function in the actual ministry to meet needs. The people with these gifts are evangelists, prophets, teachers, exhorters, pastor/shepherds, mercy showers, servers, givers, and administrators.

TEAM MINISTRY: TEAM Ministry is a philosophy of ministry centered on the believer. Every Christian has a spiritual gift and, therefore, a responsibility to function as part of the team. The gifts govern the ministry's direction and thrust. TEAM Ministry is people centered rather than task centered.

TEAM PHILOSOPHY OF MINISTRY, THE: TEAM Philosophy of Ministry: A philosophy based on using people where they are usable. It involves individuals in the work of the ministry in the area in which God has gifted each.It recognizes that the pastor's job is not to do the work of the ministry, but to lead his people in doing the work of the ministry.

THEO-METHODOLOGIST: Theo-methodologists are people whose methods have become their theology, usually because the methods work. They scripturalize the methodology rather than building methodology and philosophy on doctrine and Scripture.

THREE HEARINGS, THE PRINCIPLE OF: Research shows that when people make a decision the first time they attend church, less than one percent of them will stick to the decision. People who hear at least three presentations of the Gospel before they make a decision are more apt to make one that sticks. A hearing can be your personal testimony, a testimony of a friend, a revival service, a regular worship service, a Christmas program, a Sunday School banquet or any other event where a prospect may hear the Gospel.

WORK-FORCE ECONOMICS: Work-force economics is the act of using people where they are usable; placing Christians where their gifts are best utilized to do God's work.

BIBLIOGRAPHY

Abell, Cam and Moyer, Larry. *142 Evangelism Ideas for Your Church.* Grand Rapids, MI: Baker Book House, 1990.

Aldrich, Joseph C. *Gentle Persuasion: Creative Ways to Introduce Your Friends to Christ.* Portland, OR: Multnomah Press, 1988.

Aldrich, Joseph; Eims, LeRoy; and Hendricks, Howard. *Lifestyle Evangelism & Follow-up.* Colorado Springs, CO: NavPress, 1983.

Anderson, Leith. *Dying for Change: An Arresting Look at the New Realities Confronting Churches and Para-Church Ministries.* Minneapolis, MN: Bethany House Publishers, 1990.

Arn, Charles; McGavran, Donald; and Arn, Win. *Growth: A New Vision for the Sunday School.* Pasadena, CA: Church Growth Press, 1980.

Arn, Win and Arn, Charles. *The Master's Plan for Making Disciples.* Pasadena, CA: Church Growth Press, 1982.

Arn, Win, Dr. *The Pastor's Church Growth Handbook,* Volumes I and II. Pasadena, CA: Church Growth Press, 1982.

Arn, Win. *The Church Growth Ratio Book: How to Have a Revitalized, Healthy, Growing, Loving Church.* Pasadena, CA: Church Growth, Inc., 1987.

Arthur, Kay. *How to Discover Your Spiritual Gifts.* Chattanooga, TN: Reach Out, Inc., 1977.

Augsburger, Myron; Ratz, Calvin; and Tillapaugh, Frank. *Mastering Outreach & Evangelism.* Portland, OR: Multnomah Press, 1990.

Barna, George. *How to Find Your Church.* Minneapolis, MN: World Wide Publications, 1989.

Barna, George. *Marketing the Church: What They Never Taught You About Church Growth.* Colorado Springs, CO: NavPress, 1988.

Barna, George. *The Frog in the Kettle.* Dallas, TX: Word Publishing, 1989.

Bast, Robert L. *Attracting New Members*. Monrovia, CA and New York, NY: Church Growth, Inc. and Reformed Church in America, 1988.

Bellah, Mike. *Baby Boom Believers*. Wheaton, IL: Tyndale House Publishers, Inc., 1988.

Bittlinger, Arnold. *Gifts and Graces*. Grand Rapids, MI: William B. Eerdmans Publishing Company, 1967.

Blanchard, Tim. *A Practical Guide to Finding Your Spiritual Gifts*. Wheaton, IL: Tyndale House Publishers, Inc., 1979.

Borthwick, Paul. *Leading the Way: Leadership is Not Just For Super Christians*. Colorado Springs, CO: NavPress, 1989.

Bridge, Donald and Phypers, David. *Spiritual Gifts & The Church*. Downers Grove, IL: InterVarsity Press, 1973.

Bryson, O.J. *Networking the Kingdom: A Practical Strategy for Maximum Church Growth*. Dallas, TX: Word Publishing, 1990.

Bugbee, Bruce L. *Networking: Identifying Your Spiritual Gifts, Passion, and Temperament to Make Your Unique Contribution to the Local Church*. Pasadena, CA: Charles E. Fuller Institute, 1989.

Bullinger, E.W. *The Giver and His Gifts*. Grand Rapids, MI: Kregel Publications, 1905.

Bushey, Sharon. *The Winning Welcome: Helping Church Newcomers Feel at Home*. Kansas City, MO: Beacon Hill Press of Kansas City, 1989.

Carter, Howard. *Spiritual Gifts and Their Operation*. Springfield, MO: Gospel Publishing House, 1968.

Cathcart, Jim. *Relationship Selling: How to Get and Keep Customers*. Costa Mesa, CA: HDL Publishing, 1988.

Chappell, Paul W. *T.E.A.M. Soul Winning*. Lancaster, CA: Lancaster Baptist Publications, 1989.

Charles E. Fuller Institute. *Spiritual Gifts & Church Growth Leader's Guide*. Pasadena, CA: Charles E. Fuller Institute, 1978.

Church Development Resources. *Building Bridges: The Art and Practice of Evangelistic Calling.* Grand Rapids, MI: Church Development Resources, 1988.

Clark, Martin E. *Choosing Your Career: The Christian's Decision Manual.* Phillipsburg, NJ: Presbyterian and Reformed Publishing Co., 1981.

Clayton, Lynn P. *No Second-Class Christians.* Nashville, TN: Broadman Press, 1976.

Clinton, Bobby. *Spiritual Gifts.* Coral Gables, FL: Learning Resource Center Publications, 1975.

Coleman, Robert E. *The Master Plan of Evangelism.* Old Tappan, NJ: Fleming H. Revell, 1964.

Corle, Dennis A. *Reaching the World One Door at a Time.* 1986.

Dale, Robert D. *To Dream Again.* Nashville, TN: Broadman Press, 1981.

David C. Cook Publishing Co. *Congratulations-You're Gifted.* Elgin, IL: David C. Cook Publishing Co., 1975.

Davis, Bob C., Dr. *Building A Soul Winning Church.* Concord, VA: personal publication, 1975.

Dillon, William S. *God's Work in God's Way.* Woodworth, WI: Brown Gold Publications, 1957.

Dubose, Francis M.; Hadaway, Kirk C.; and Wright, Stuart A. *Home Cell Groups and House Churches.* Nashville, TN: Broadman Press, 1987.

Edwards, Gene. *How to Have a Soul Winning Church.* Springfield, MO: Gospel Publishing House, 1963.

Engstrom, Ted W. *Your Gift of Administration: How to Discover and Use It.* Nashville, TN: Thomas Nelson Publishers, 1979.

Epp, Theodore H. *Spiritual Gifts for Every Believer.* Lincoln, NE: Back to the Bible, 1962.

Finzel, Hans. *Help! I'm A Baby Boomer*. Wheaton, IL: Victor Books, 1989.

Fowler, Harry H. *Breaking Barriers of New Church Growth*. Rocky Mount, NC: Creative Growth Dynamics, 1988.

Galloway, Dale E. 20/20 Vision: *How to Create a Successful Church With Lay Pastors and Cell Groups*. Portland, OR: Scott Publishing Co., 1986.

Gangel, Kenneth O. *Unwrap Your Spiritual Gifts*. Wheaton, IL: Victor Books, 1983.

Gangel, Kenneth O. *You and Your Spiritual Gifts*. Chicago, IL: Moody Press, 1975.

Gee, Donald. *Concerning Spiritual Gifts*. Springfield, MO: Radiant Books, 1949.

Gee, Donald. *Spiritual Gifts in the Work of the Ministry Today*. Springfield, MO: Gospel Publishing House, 1963.

George, Carl F. and Logan, Robert E. *Leading & Managing Your Church*. Old Tappan, NJ: Fleming H. Revell Co., 1987.

Gordon, A.J. *The Ministry of the Spirit*. Minneapolis, MN: Bethany Fellowship, Inc., 1964.

Graham, Billy. *The Holy Spirit Activating God's Power In Your Life*. Waco, TX: Word Books, 1978.

Griffin, Em. *Making Friends (& Making Them Count)*. Downers Grove, IL: InterVarsity Press, 1987.

Griswold, Roland E. *The Winning Church*. Wheaton, IL: Victor Books, 1986.

Grooms, J.O. *Soul-Winners Paradise*. Lynchburg, VA: Treasure Path to Soul-Winning, Inc., 1978.

Grooms, J.O. *Treasure Path to Soul -Winning*. Lynchburg, VA: Treasure Path to Soul-Winning, Inc., 1978.

Hartman, Warren J. *Five Audiences: Identifying Groups in Your Church*. Nashville, TN: Abingdon Press, 1987.

Hauck, Gary L. *Is My Church What God Meant It to Be*. Denver, CO: Accent B/P Publications, 1979.

Hendrix, Olan. *Management for the Christian Leader*. Grand Rapids, MI: Baker Book House, 1981.

Hickey, Marilyn. *Seven Gifts to Success*. Denver, CO: Life for Laymen, Inc. 1976.

Hind, James F. *The Heart & Soul of Effective Management*. Wheaton, IL: Victor Books, 1989.

Hinkle, James and Woodroof, Tim. *Among Friends: You Can Help Make Your Church a Warmer Place*. Colorado Springs, CO: NavPress, 1989.

Hunter, Kent R. *6 Faces of the Christian Church: How to Light a Fire in a Lukewarm Church*. Corunna, IN: Church Growth Center, 1983.

Hunter, Kent R. *Foundations for Church Growth*. New Haven, MO: Leader Publishing Co., 1983.

Hunter, Kent R. *Gifted for Growth: An Implementation Guide for Mobilizing the Laity*. Corunna, IN: Church Growth Center, 1985.

Hunter, Kent R. *Launching Growth in the Local Congregation*. Corunna, IN: Church Growth Center, 1981.

Hunter, Kent R. *Your Church Has Doors: How to Open the Front and Close the Back*. Corunna, IN: Church Growth Analysis and Learning Center, 1982.

Hunter, Kent R. *Your Church Has Personality*. Nashville, TN: Abingdon Press, 1985.

Hurn, Raymond W., Dr. *Finding Your Ministry*. Kansas City, MO: Beacon Hill Press of Kansas City, 1979.

Hutchins, Clair Dean and Gibson, Brother John. *Winning the World*. St. Petersburg, FL: World Mission Crusade, 1985.

Innes, Dick. *I Hate Witnessing*. Ventura, CA: Vision House, 1983.

Institute For American Church Growth. *How to Mobilize Your Laity for Ministry Through Your Church.* Pasadena, CA: Institute for American Church Growth.

Institute For American Church Growth. *Spiritual Gifts for Building the Body.* Pasadena, CA: Institute for American Church Growth, 1979.

Jenson, Ron and Stevens, Jim. *Dynamics of Church Growth.* Grand Rapids, MI: Baker Book House, 1981.

Jones, Landon Y. *Great Expectations: America and the Baby Boom Generation.* New York, NY: Ballantine Books, 1980.

Kennedy, D. James. *Evangelism Explosion.* Wheaton IL: Tyndale House Publishers, 1977.

Kilinski, Kenneth K. and Wofford, Jerry C. *Organization and Leadership in the Local Church.* Grand Rapids, MI: Zondervan Publishing House, 1973.

Kimble, R.L. *Spread the Gospel.* Greensboro, NC: Spread the Gospel.

LeTourneau, R.G. *Mover of Men and Mountains.* Chicago, IL: Moody Press. 1960.

Light, Paul C. *Baby Boomers.* New York, NY: W.W. Norton & Company, Inc., 1988.

Little, Paul E. *How to Give Away Your Faith.* Downers Grove, IL: InterVarsity Press, 1966.

Logan, Robert E. *Beyond Church Growth: Action Plans for Developing a Dynamic Church.* Old Tappan, NJ: Fleming H. Revell Co., 1989.

Lord, Jack. *Evangelism Person to Person.* Personal publication.

Lovett, C.S. *Visitation Made Easy.* Baldwin Park, CA: Personal Christianity, 1959.

Lovett, C.S. *Witnessing Made Easy.* Baldwin Park, CA: Personal Christianity, 1971.

Mattson, Ralph and Miller, Arthur. *Finding a Job You Can Love*. Nashville, TN: Thomas Nelson Publishers, 1982.

Mattson, Ralph T. and Miller, Arthur F. *The Truth about You: Discover What You Should Be Doing With Your Life*. Old Tappan, NJ: Fleming H. Revell Co., 1977.

Maxwell, John C. *Be A People Person*. Wheaton, IL: Victor Books, 1989.

Maxwell, John C., Dr. *Biblically Teaching Spiritual Gifts*. San Diego, CA.

May, F.J. *The Book of Acts & Church Growth: Growth Through the Power of God's Holy Spirit*. Cleveland, TN: Pathway Press, 1990.

McDill, Wayne. *Making Friends for Christ – A Practical Approach to Relational Evangelism*. Nashville, TN: Broadman Press, 1979.

McMinn, Gordon N., Ph.D. *Spiritual Gifts Inventory*. Portland, OR: Western Baptist Press, 1978.

Miller, Arthur F. and Mattson, Ralph T. *The Truth about You*. Old Tappan, NJ: Fleming H. Revell Company, 1977.

Mueller, Walter. *Direct Mail Ministry: Evangelism, Stewardship, Caregiving*. Nashville, TN: Abingdon Press, 1989.

Murren, Doug. *The Baby Boomerang: Catching Baby Boomers as They Return to Church*. Ventura, CA: Regal Books, 1990.

Neighbour, Ralph W., Jr. *The Touch of the Spirit: The Spirit-filled Approach to Witnessing*. Nashville, TN: Broadman Press, 1972.

Neighbour, Ralph W., Jr. *This Gift is Mine*. Nashville, TN: Broadman Press, 1974.

Palmer, John M. *Equipping for Ministry*. Springfield, MO: Gospel Publishing House, 1985.

Parrish, Archie and John. *Best Friends: Developing An Intimate Relationship With God*. Waco, TX: Word, Inc., 1984.

Parrish, Archie. *The Chinese Secret Witnessing Kit*. Atlanta, GA: SERVE International, 1988.

Petersen, Jim. *Evangelism as a Lifestyle: Reaching Into Your World With the Gospel.* Colorado Springs, CO: NavPress, 1987.

Petersen, Jim. *Evangelism for Our Generation.* Colorado Springs, CO: NavPress, 1985.

Petersen, Jim. *Evangelism for Our Generation: The Practical Way to Make Evangelism Your Lifestyle.* Colorado Springs, CO: NavPress, 1985.

Prange, Erwin E. *The Gift Is Already Yours.* Minneapolis, MN: Bethany Fellowship, Inc., 1980.

Rice, John R. *Prayer: Asking and Receiving.* Murfreesboro, TN: Sword of the Lord Publishers, 1942.

Rice, John R. *The Golden Path to Successful Personal Soul Winning.* Wheaton, IL: Sword of the Lord Publishers, 1961.

Rice, John R., Dr. *How Great Soul Winners Were Filled With The Holy Spirit.* Murfreesboro, TN: Sword of The Lord Publishers, 1949.

Ries, Al and Trout, Jack. *Positioning: The Battle for Your Mind.* New York, NY: McGraw-Hill Book Co., 1986.

Rueter, Alvin C. *Organizing for Evangelism: Planning an Effective Program for Witnessing.* Minneapolis, MN: Augsburg Publishing House, 1983.

Rush, Myron. *Management: A Biblical Approach.* Wheaton, IL: Victor Books, 1989.

Rush, Myron. *Managing to Be the Best: A Personal Approach.* Wheaton, IL: Victor Books, 1989.

Rush, Myron. *The New Leader: A Revolutionary Approach to Effective Leadership.* Wheaton, IL: Victor Books, 1989.

Rusthoi, Ralph W. *Harvesting for Christ.* Montrose, CA: Soul Winning Publications, 1969.

Salter, Darius. *What Really Matters in Ministry: Profiling Pastoral Success in Flourishing Churches.* Grand Rapids, MI: Baker Book House, 1990.

Schaller, Lyle E. *44 Ways to Increase Church Attendance*. Nashville, TN: Abingdon Press, 1988.

Schaller, Lyle E. *Reflections of a Contrarian*. Nashville, TN: Abingdon Press, 1989.

Schaller, Lyle E. *The Multiple Staff and the Larger Church*. Nashville, TN: Abingdon Press, 1980.

Schuller, Robert H. *Self Esteem: The New Reformation*. Waco, TX: Word Books, 1982.

Senter, Mark, III. *The Art of Recruiting Volunteers*. Wheaton, IL: Victor Books, 1960.

Sisson, Dick. *Evangelism Encounter: Bringing the Excitement of Evangelism Back into the Body*. Wheaton, IL: Victor Books, 1988.

Slocum, Robert E. *Maximize Your Ministry*. Colorado Springs, CO: NavPress, 1990.

Stedman, Ray C. *A Study Guide for Body Life*. Glendale, CA: Regal Books, 1977.

Stedman, Ray C. *Body Life*. Glendale, CA: Regal Books, 1972.

Stott, John. *One People: Helping Your Church Become a Caring Community*. Harrisburg, PA: Christian Publications, Inc., 1982.

Sullivan, Bill M. *Ten Steps to Breaking the 200 Barrier*. Kansas City, MO: Beacon Hill Press of Kansas City, 1988.

Terry, Lindsay. *How to Build an Evangelistic Church Music Program*. Nashville, TN: Thomas Nelson, Inc. , 1974.

The Sunday School Board of the Southern Baptist Convention. *Discovering Your Spiritual Gifts*. Nashville, TN: The Sunday School Board of the Southern Baptist Convention, 1981.

Towns, Elmer L. *An Inside Look at 10 of Todays's Most Innovative Churches*. Ventura, CA: Regal Books, 1984.

Towns, Elmer L. *Becoming a Leader*. Lynchburg, VA: Church Growth Institute, 1986.

Towns, Elmer L. *How to Grow An Effective Sunday School.* Lynchburg, VA: Church Growth Institute, 1987.

Towns, Elmer. *154 Steps to Revitalize Your Sunday School and Keep Your Church Growing.* Wheaton, IL: Victor Books, 1988.

Towns, Elmer. *Friends.* Lynchburg, VA: Church Growth Institute, 1989.

Towns, Elmer. *How to Reach Your Friends for Christ.* Lynchburg, VA: Church Growth Institute, 1989.

Towns, Elmer. *Winning the Winnable.* Lynchburg, VA: Church Growth Institute, 1989.

Tozer, A.W. *Tragedy in the Church: The Missing Gifts.* Harrisburg, PA: Christian Publications, Inc., 1978.

Van Auken, Philip M. *The Well-Managed Ministry: Discovering & Developing the Strengths of Your Team.* Wheaton, IL: Victor Books, 1989.

Van Der Puy, Abe C. *The High Calling of God: You Can Serve Successfully.* Lincoln, NE: Back to the Bible, 1982.

Vaughan, John N. *The Large Church: A Twentieth-Century Expression of the First-Century Church.* Grand Rapids, MI: Baker Book House, 1985.

Vaughan, John N. *The World's 20 Largest Churches: Church Growth Principles in Action.* Grand Rapids, MI: Baker Book House, 1986.

Wagner, C. Peter. *Church Growth State of the Art.* Wheaton, IL: Tyndale House Publishers, Inc., 1986.

Wagner, C. Peter. *Leading Your Church to Growth.* Ventura, CA: Regal Books, 1984.

Wagner, C. Peter. *Spiritual Power and Church Growth.* Altamonte Springs, FL: Strang Communications Co., 1986.

Wagner, C. Peter. *Your Church Can Be Healthy.* Nashville, TN: Abingdon, 1979.

Wagner, C. Peter. *Your Church Can Grow*. Glendale, CA: Regal Books, 1976.

Wagner, C. Peter. *Your Spiritual Gifts Can Help Your Church Grow*. Glendale, CA: Regal Books, 1979.

Wagner, Stephen. *Heart to Heart: Sharing Christ with a Friend*. Corunna, IN: Church Growth Center, 1985.

Watts, Wayne. *The Gift of Giving*. Colorado Springs, CO: NavPress, 1982.

Webley, Simon. *How to Give Away Your Money*. Downers Grove, IL: InterVarsity Press, 1978.

Wemp, C. Sumner. *How on Earth Can I Be Spiritual?* Nashville, TN: Thomas Nelson Inc., 1978.

Werning, Waldo J. *Vision and Strategy for Church Growth*. Chicago, IL: Moody Press, 1977.

White, Ernest. *The Art of Human Relations*. Nashville, TN: Broadman Press, 1985.

White, Jerry and Mary. *Friends Friendship: The Secrets of Drawing Closer*. Colorado Springs, CO: NavPress, 1982.

Willis, Avery T., Jr. *MasterLife II Discipleship Training*. Nashville, TN: The Sunday School Board of the Southern Baptist Convention, 1985.

Willmington, Harold. *The Doctrine of the Holy Spirit*. Lynchburg, VA: personal publication.

Wimber, John and Springer, Kevin. *Power Evangelism*. San Francisco, CA: Harper & Row, Publishers, 1986.

Winslow, Octavius. *The Work of the Holy Spirit*. Carlisle, PA: The Banner of Truth Trust, 1840.

Yohn, Rick. *Discover Your Spiritual Gift and Use It*. Wheaton, IL: Tyndale House Publishers, Inc., 1974.

ORDER FORM

Quant.	Item #	Product Name	Price per Item	Total	Info. only (No charge)
	407T	*TEAM Evangelism* textbooks (contains 2 Spiritual Gifts answer sheets, 1 *TEAM Mate* booklet)	9.95		☐
	112	*TEAM Ministry* textbooks (includes Spiritual Gifts Inventory)	9.95		☐
	407M 407Y	*TEAM Mate* Personal Ministry Planners Adult Version Youth Version (with free Leader's Guide) 1-25 copies, $2.00 ea. 26 or more, $1.49 ea.			☐ ☐
	401S 401X	*Spiritual Gifts Inventory* (Questionnaire & Answer Sheet) English Edition (min. order of 10) Spanish Edition (min. order of 10) 1-9 copies, $2.50 ea. 10-49 copies, $2.00 ea. 50-99 copies, $1.50 ea. 100 or more, $1.25 ea.			☐ ☐
	407	*TEAM Evangelism* Resource Packets	99.95		☐
	407W	*TEAM Evangelism* Student Workbooks	2.95		☐
	405	*TEAM Ministry* Resource Packets	79.95		☐
	405L	*TEAM Ministry* Lapel Pins 25-49 pins,.75 ea.; 50-99, .65 ea. 100 or more, .60 ea.			☐
	615	*Night of Caring* Video Packet	149.95		☐
	614	*Outreach Bible Study* Packet	149.95		☐
	613	*Living Proof* Video Packet	179.95		☐

TOTAL ORDER

Shipping ($5.50 USA, $6.50 Canada)

Amount Enclosed

Check One:

☐ Pastor   ☐ Assoc. Pastor   ☐ C.E. Director   ☐ Layperson   ☐ S.S. Teacher

Name_____ Church _____

Address_____ City_____

State _____ Zip_____ Phone_____

Payment must accompany order.   **Send order to:** **Church Growth Institute**

Please allow 2-3 weeks for delivery.

Providing Practical Tools for Growth
P.O. Box 4404, Lynchburg, VA 24502

ORDER FORM

Quant.	Item #	Product Name	Price per Item	Total	Info. only (No charge)
	407T	*TEAM Evangelism* textbooks (contains 2 Spiritual Gifts answer sheets, 1 *TEAM Mate* booklet)	9.95		☐
	112	*TEAM Ministry* textbooks (includes Spiritual Gifts Inventory)	9.95		☐
	407M 407Y	**TEAM Mate** **Personal Ministry Planners** Adult Version Youth Version (with free Leader's Guide) 1-25 copies, $2.00 ea. 26 or more, $1.49 ea.			☐ ☐
	401S 401X	*Spiritual Gifts Inventory* (Questionnaire & Answer Sheet) English Edition (min. order of 10) Spanish Edition (min. order of 10) 1-9 copies, $2.50 ea. 10-49 copies, $2.00 ea. 50-99 copies, $1.50 ea. 100 or more, $1.25 ea.			☐ ☐
	407	*TEAM Evangelism* Resource Packets	99.95		☐
	407W	*TEAM Evangelism* Student Workbooks	2.95		☐
	405	*TEAM Ministry* Resource Packets	79.95		☐
	405L	*TEAM Ministry* Lapel Pins 25-49 pins,.75 ea.; 50-99, .65 ea. 100 or more, .60 ea.			☐
	615	*Night of Caring* Video Packet	149.95		☐
	614	*Outreach Bible Study* Packet	149.95		☐
	613	*Living Proof* Video Packet	179.95		☐

TOTAL ORDER

Shipping ($5.50 USA, $6.50 Canada)

Amount Enclosed

Check One:

☐ Pastor   ☐ Assoc. Pastor   ☐ C.E. Director   ☐ Layperson   ☐ S.S. Teacher

Name_____ Church _____

Address_____ City_____

State _____ Zip_____ Phone_____

Payment must accompany order.   **Send order to:**   **Church Growth Institute**

Please allow 2-3 weeks for delivery.

Providing Practical Tools for Growth
P.O. Box 4404, Lynchburg, VA 24502

A lot of team effort was involved in developing this *TEAM Evangelism* text and resource packet. Various members participated in planning, writing, editing, designing, printing, assembling, shipping, promoting, and processing orders for this exciting new resource. Hats off to our hardworking team who produced *TEAM Evangelism*. We pray that your team will extend our efforts and use *TEAM Evangelism* to reach others for Christ.